GOODCHRISTIANS
GOODHUSBANDS?

Resourced by thorough research into the marriages of Wesley, Whitefield and Edwards, this is a truly wise book on the problem of combining ministry and marriage to the glory of God and the good of all concerned.

J. I. Packer,
Professor of Theology, Regent College, Vancouver, Canada

Doreen Moore has done more than write a typical book on marriage. She has seen the impact of life itself upon real people who had real needs and real struggles. The result is a wonderful blend of biography and helpful insight into how God works in our marriages for his kingdom's advance through weak and unworthy servants.

John Armstrong,
Founder and President of Reformation and Revival Ministries

Driven by a confluence of four motivations, Doreen Moore has produced a study of marriage that is helpful and charming. She is a good historian. I remember this from excellent work that she did in the history program at Trinity Evangelical Divinity School. Her desire for accurate helpful history gives energy to the historical investigation of the three highly pertinent examples of how evangelical 'calling' impacts to the marriage relationship. She is a concerned theologian. Marriage as a part of the divine order and a subject of divine revelation has an important part in a comprehensive display of God's purpose in the world. She has been careful to give it a theological arrangement. She is a wife. She understands the pressures brought to bear on a marriage by intense ministry goals and demands. Developing a deep sense of the stewardship of marriage is important to her and helps as her argument unfolds. She is a mother. The mysterious union achieved in a family through the begetting of children and rearing them in the nurture and admonition of the Lord is both a personal experience and a theological truth for her. Christian Focus should be congratulated for the pursuit of this manuscript by Doreen and each reader will receive rewards in personal development far in excess of the time invested in reading.

Tom J. Nettles
Professor of Historical Theology,
The Southern Baptist Theological Seminary, Louisville, KY

Outstanding analysis of the tensions between marriage and ministry and how the two need not be competitors. Very well worth the reading.

Dwight Edwards,
Senior Pastor, Grace Bible Church, College Station, TX

GOODCHRISTIANS GOODHUSBANDS?

Leaving a Legacy in Marriage & Ministry

Lessons from the marriages & ministries of
Elizabeth & George Whitefield
Sarah & Jonathan Edwards
Molly & John Wesley

Doreen Moore

CHRISTIAN FOCUS

Copyright © Doreen Moore 2004

ISBN 1-85792-450-9

Published in 2004
by
Christian Focus Publications,
Geanies House,Fearn,
Ross-shire, IV20 1TW, Scotland

www.christianfocus.com

Cover design by Alister MacInnes

Printed and bound by
Cox & Wyman, Reading, Berkshire

Contents

Acknowledgements:

To my Lord and Savior Jesus Christ, of whom Jonathan Edwards said is "worthy, that we should serve Him to the utmost of our power in all things."

To my husband, Dave – for being my nearest and dearest partner in life and ministry. Thank you for all you do and say to draw me closer to Christ. Thank you too for all your encouragement and editorial assistance.

To my sons, David and Christopher – you have brought so much joy into my life. I love who God has made you. My life is richer and a whole lot more fun because of you. I love being your mother!

To my mother and father – for all your encouragement. I am especially grateful that you created an environment where I always knew I was loved. I also am grateful that you have encouraged me to seek to excel at whatever I do.

To Dr. Woodbridge and Dr. Nettles – Thank you for making church history come alive. Dr. Woodbridge, I am indebted to you for teaching me the skills of historiography.

To my publishers – in a day and age when many seek only to entertain the sheep, I thank you for being faithful to feed the sheep. A special thank you to my editor, Anne. May God bless you richly in your new ministry as a mom (Isa. 40:11).

To my many friends and co-laborers in ministry who have devoted their lives to the glory of God and the well-being of others – especially Darin and Allison Maurer, Brooke and Karen Butler, Mike and Marlena Rupp, Lore and Michael Cooper, Linda and Dennis Ryan, Kurt and Susie Richardson, and Tsh and Kyle Oxenreider. Though the world thinks we are making a sacrifice, we know that a life lived in service and love to God is the best life one could have.

To my Austin friends who have provided ongoing encouragement and prayers over the years. A special thank you to my friend, Vickie Hooper, for her never ending supply of encouragement. Jane and Denise, your prayers held me up. Thank you to the Rogan family for a computer.

Thank you to everyone who expressed interest in the book. It doesn't take a village – it takes a Body – the Body of Christ!

I am a blessed woman!

Introduction

When C. T. Studd[1] felt that the Lord was calling him to Africa as a missionary, his wife Priscilla objected. It was not that she was not committed to missions. In fact, she had been a missionary in China when he met her, actively involved in people's lives. However, Priscilla now had a serious heart condition and could not go with him. Despite her feelings, he left her. She was devastated. Even when her heart problems grew worse, he did not return. In Africa, he worked eighteen hours a day, with "no diversions, no days off, no recreation."[2] In his zeal, he expected his co-laborers to do the same. This caused strained relationships with the other missionaries. He even dismissed his own daughter and son-in-law because they failed to meet his standards. C. T. Studd believed "the cause of Christ" took precedence over his family.

When William Carey, the father of modern missions, decided to go to India as a missionary, his wife refused to go. She had three children and was pregnant with a fourth. He resolved to go even if he had to leave her and the children behind. Shortly after the birth of her fourth child she gave in and accompanied him to India.[3] What followed was a nightmare for her. It started with a five month sea voyage where she was seasick most of the time.[4] When they arrived in Calcutta, their inadequate funds were quickly depleted, forcing his family to live in a rundown place outside of Calcutta.[5] Even worse, the other missionaries lived in relative affluence in Calcutta. His wife complained because they had to "live without many of . . .the necessaries of life, bread in particular."[6] Dorothy was also afflicted with dysentery and their oldest son almost died from it. Later, Carey moved his wife, infant, and three sons under ten, into an untamed malarial infested region where alligators, tigers, and huge poisonous snakes were in abundance.[7] They moved soon after to Mudnabatti, where Dorothy again became ill. But far worse, their five year old son Peter died.[8] After this devastating loss, Dorothy Carey's mental health declined. She never recovered but deteriorated to such an extent that she was described as "wholly deranged."[9] William Carey believed "the cause of Christ" took precedence over his family.

When David Livingstone undertook his missionary journeys to Africa, his wife Mary and their children accompanied him. His wife had been raised as a missionary kid and was accustomed to hardship. On the first journey together, their newborn daughter died from lack of water,[10] the other child almost died, and Mary suffered temporary paralysis.[11] Livingstone realized the rigors of an exploratory lifestyle were too hard on his family.[12] Seven years into their marriage he decided to send Mary and their four children[13] to Scotland to live with his parents.[14] He would remain in Africa and continue his explorations. He wrote how this "act of orphanising" his children was painful to him because they would not remember him.[15] Yet he based his decision on a "strong conviction that this step will tend to the Glory of Christ."[16] While Livingstone dreamed of seeing the end of the African slave trade and discovering the source of the Nile (to verify Biblical accuracy),[17] his family lived close to the poverty level. It seems likely that Livingstone's wife became an alcoholic to deal with depression.[18] She begged him to return, but he wouldn't.[19] When Livingstone finally did return to England he was welcomed as a hero and received a gold medal from the Royal Geographic Society.[20] He later wrote how his time in England "was so busy that I could not enjoy much the company of my children."[21] On his next journey, Mary refused to be left behind even though this would be a dangerous journey. She left her children, including a newborn, behind with Livingstone's relatives.[22] Three months later, after having been "pushed ... beyond human endurance"[23] by her husband, Mary Livingstone died of malaria.[24] In 17 years of marriage, they had only lived together for 4 years.[25] David Livingstone believed "the cause of Christ" took precedence over his family.

Throughout the history of the Christian church and even today, similar stories could be told. Other great men, who had extensive influence in their labors for "the cause of Christ," believed that their public ministry took precedence over their families. These men followed the course they believed God had called them to follow and expected their wives and children to follow as well. These men had a passion to spread the gospel and change the social evils of the cultures to which they went. We admire, for example, William Carey's dedication to seeing sati (widow burning) and infanticide banned from India.[26] We admire the extent of his translation work. He translated the Bible into six languages and parts of it were translated into twenty-nine other languages.[27] Yet it is difficult not to have angst over his domestic relationships. Should he have been a missionary? Could there have been anything he could have done to ease some of the hardships?

This raises many questions regarding the relationship between one's marriage and one's ministry outside the home. For instance, does one aspect of ministry (i.e. ministry to family versus ministry to the world) have priority over the other? If a man believes he is "called" to a particular ministry outside the home (e.g. to be a missionary, pastor, etc.), is his wife to accept this regardless of how she feels? Could her reticence be a sign that perhaps God is not calling that man into such a ministry? On the other hand, is it not possible that undue concern over family matters can become idolatrous? And perhaps the question that encompasses all the others is: what biblical and theological convictions should govern how one views one's role as a minister of the gospel in relation to one's role as a husband and father?[28] How a person answers these questions has serious ramifications for both his family and his ministry. These questions are not to be taken lightly.

In trying to come to godly convictions regarding the relationship between one's family and one's ministry, it is helpful to look historically at those who have made what is deemed a significant contribution to the cause of Christ to see what biblical and theological convictions governed their lives. For this task I have chosen three prominent eighteenth-century Christian leaders: John Wesley, George Whitefield, and Jonathan Edwards. We will see how they viewed their ministerial responsibilities in relation to their responsibilities as husbands and/or fathers. All three of these men were married and all three were leaders during a unique time in Christian history when surely it was incumbent on ministers to "spend and be spent" for the work of ministry. This time was known in England as the English Evangelical Revival, in Scotland as the Scottish Cambuslang Wark, and in America as the First Great Awakening. Scholars today acknowledge it as one great intercontinental revival that spanned England, Scotland, Wales, and America. John Wesley, George Whitefield, and Jonathan Edwards all played a significant part in this great revival. A brief biographical sketch of each will demonstrate their commitment to Christ and to the work of Christ.

John Wesley was born on June 17, 1703 in Epworth, England.[29] When he was five years old, a fire broke out in his home and his was a near miraculous rescue. He later viewed himself as a "brand plucked from the fire" (Zech. 3:2). It seemed Providence spared him for a unique destiny.[30] He devoted himself to God and to good works, even going on a mission trip to Georgia (America). His personal failure while in Georgia prompted him to record in his journal that "I who went to America to convert others, was never myself converted to God."[31] It was only after he returned to England that he went to a prayer meeting at Aldersgate and heard Luther's preface on the Epistle to the Romans. He wrote of this experience, "About a quarter before nine, while he was describing the change which God works in the heart through faith in Christ, I felt my heart strangely warmed. I felt I did trust in Christ, Christ alone for salvation: And an assurance was given me, that he had taken away *my* sins, even *mine*, and saved *me* from the law of sin and death."[32] Soon after, Wesley began itinerating and preaching salvation by grace through faith alone. Revival broke out and lasted until he died. For fifty-two years he travelled as an itinerant minister, averaging 4,500 miles yearly and a total of 40,000 sermons.[33] Wesley was committed to reforming the social evils that plagued his society as well. Poverty, slavery, and prison reform, for example, were issues to which he was committed.[34] He later broke with the Church of England and founded the Methodist denomination.[35] He labored until he died in 1791.[36] John Wesley's desire was to "spend and be spent" for the work of Christ.

George Whitefield was born in Gloucester, England on December 16, 1714.[37] The sins of his youth, he said, were endless yet he also remembers the Spirit stirring in his heart.[38] When he went to Oxford, he met Charles Wesley. Wesley gave Whitefield a copy of *The Life of God in the Soul of Man* by Henry Scougal.[39] It was in this excellent treatise that Whitefield discovered that "true religion was union of the soul with God, and Christ formed within us."[40] Whitefield wrote, "a ray of Divine light was instantaneously darted in upon my soul, and from that moment, but not till then, did I know that I must be a new creature."[41] From that moment on Whitefield's sole desire was to live for the glory of God. All he desired was to tell people about Christ and that "there was such a thing as the new birth."[42] Two years later, in 1737, he was ordained in the Church of England.[43] He later became an itinerant evangelist and traveled to Scotland, Wales, Ireland, America, and throughout England as well.[44] Many attribute the interconnectedness of the revival to this great preacher.[45] He preached close to 18,000 sermons in his thirty-four years of public ministry.[46] He also established an orphan-house in Georgia.[47] He died in 1770,[48] his body literally worn out from his extensive labors. George Whitefield's desire was to "spend and be spent" for the work of Christ.

Jonathan Edwards was born on October 5, 1703, in Windsor Connecticut.[49] He was raised in a godly home.[50] Later on, he wrote regarding his testimony, "The first instance, that I remember, of that sort of inward, sweet delight in God and divine things, that I have lived much in since, was on reading those words, 1 Tim. i. 17. *Now unto the King eternal, immortal, invisible, the only wise God, be honour and glory for ever and ever. Amen.* As I read the words, there came into my soul, and was as it were diffused through it, a sense of the glory of the Divine Being; a new sense, quite different from any thing I ever experienced before."[51] From that time on his "sense of divine things" kept increasing. On January 12, 1723, he wrote a dedication of himself to God, "giving up myself, and all that I had, to God;

to be for the future in no respect my own; to act as one that had no right to himself, in any respect. And so solemnly vowed to take God for my portion and felicity, looking on nothing else as any part of my happiness, nor acting as it were; and his law for the constant rule of my obedience; engaging to fight with all my might against the world, the flesh, and the devil, to the end of my life."[52] Not only did Jonathan Edwards grow in his godliness, but his mental powers were also used for the glory of God, prompting even secular scholars to acknowledge that Edwards was the greatest thinker America ever produced. During the Great Awakening, this Congregational minister and theologian, pastored a church in Northampton, Massachusetts.[53] He reported that when revival broke out in his church, there were over three hundred converts.[54] While pastoring, he also wrote many works on the revival.[55] By the late 1740s he was dismissed from his congregation because of some doctrinal differences.[56] He moved his family to Stockbridge where they labored among the Indians.[57] Edwards also wrote some of his finest theological treatises in that ten year period.[58] He later was asked to be the president of the College of New Jersey (now known as Princeton).[59] In 1758, before he could begin his work there, he died from a smallpox inoculation.[60] Edwards had resolved, "Never to lose one moment of time,"[61] and never to do anything unless it brought glory to God.[62] Jonathan Edwards' desire was to "spend and be spent" for the work of Christ.

As the reader can see, all three of these men were wholeheartedly and unreservedly committed to their ministries. All three were also married and faced the same tension regarding balancing (or not balancing) marriage/family and public ministry.

This issue is not just theoretical for my husband and me. We have both been in vocational Christian ministry since graduation from college. Independently of one another, before we even met, we had committed our lives to the ministry. When we married, we dedicated ourselves together to the ministry. Children came along and the issue became more important. Our love for our children and our love for the people we are called to serve, plus the sobering reality that we answer to God, make this issue even more acute. My husband and I have had countless conversations with others over this issue. We have heard different perspectives on balancing marriage/family and public ministry. Some wives embrace the ministry. Others struggle deeply. Friends of mine who have been "ministry kids" have shared their stories with me. Some have deep scars from neglect, others have expressed how they loved growing up in a ministry home.

The Scriptures command God's workmen to "handle accurately the Word of truth" (II Tim. 2:15) and to "pay close attention" to our lives and to our teaching (I Tim. 4:16). We are to "approve the things that are excellent" (Phil. 1:10). We are to be "an example of those who believe" (I Tim. 4:12). In light of this, the purpose of this book will be to help us develop Biblical convictions regarding one's relationship to ministry in light of having a wife (and in Jonathan Edwards' case, a family as well). The

Scriptures tell us of those who have "a zeal for God, but not in accordance with knowledge" (Rom. 10:2). This book hopes to bring knowledge to our zeal, light to our passion.

The format of this book will be to devote one chapter to each person, looking at four specific areas. These areas are: the biblical and theological convictions of each of these men regarding their role and responsibilities as ministers of the gospel; the biblical and theological convictions of each of these men regarding their role and responsibilities as husbands and/or fathers; how their biblical and theological convictions shaped their actual marriages and/or families; and, how each wife responded to her husband's convictions.

The last chapter will be the conclusion. I will summarize the three perspectives and propose guidelines drawn from Scripture and some modern day "greats."

My prayer is that God will give us wisdom in the knowledge of Him and His ways! I also pray that our lives will bear much fruit for His glory, for the well-being of others, and for our own eternal joy!

If any man would learn to pray (the proverb says) let him go to sea. I say, if any man would learn to pray, let him think of marrying ... No one step or action in life has so much influence on eternity as marriage. It is an heaven or an hell (they say) in this world; much more so in the next.

Charles Wesley, 1782

Chapter One

The Marriage of John Wesley

On February 18th or 19th, 1751, John Wesley married Molly Vazeille, a merchant's widow.[1] She had been left with four children[2] and a fortune of £10,000.[3] The marriage had been hasty. Little is known of their relationship until we hear on February 2, 1751 of Wesley's resolve to marry and the woman was Molly Vazeille.[4] Just days later on February 10, intending to go north the next day, he slipped on London Bridge hitting the bone of his ankle on top of a stone. He convalesced on Threadneedle Street, where Molly Vazeille lived. The next week, he spent "partly in prayer, reading, and conversation, partly in writing a *Hebrew Grammar* and *Lessons for Children*."[5] At the end of the week they were married. John does not even mention it in his Journal! Less than two years later, Vincent Perronet, Vicar of Shoreham and close friend of both Wesley brothers, wrote to Charles Wesley concerning John's marriage:

> I am truly concerned that matters are in so melancholy a situation. I think the unhappy lady is

most to be pitied, though the gentleman's case is mournful enough. Their sufferings proceed from widely different causes. His are the visible chastisements of a loving Father, hers, the immediate effects of an angry, bitter spirit; and, indeed, it is a sad consideration, that, after so many months have elapsed, the same warmth and bitterness should remain [Nov. 3, 1752].[6]

It was indeed sad that soon after they wed, marriage became a great trial for both John and Molly Wesley. Although there were short, intermittent periods of happiness, overall the struggles were acute and the marriage proved to be uncongenial. Both sides claimed innocence and accused the other. In 1761, John wrote to James Rouquet claiming her case was "proper lunacy; but it is a preternatural, a diabolical lunacy, and therefore at those times (I know what I say) I do not think my life is safe with her" [March 30, 1761].[7] She later said she saw herself as "a poor, weak woman alone against a formidable body" and pleaded with him to "put a stop to this torrent of evil that is poured against me. It is cruel to make me an offender for defending myself. If you or any others have anything to lay to my charge, let it be proved" [May 31, 1774].[8]

In 1771, the situation had become so grievous that Molly left John. This was not the first time she left him, but it was the first time he did not ask her to return. He wrote in his Journal, "For what cause I know not to this day, – set out for Newcastle purposing 'never to return'. Non eam reliqui; non dimisi; non revocabo (I have not left her; I have not sent her away; I will not recall her)" [Jan. 23, 1771].[9]

As one looks at the life and writings of John Wesley, it becomes difficult to understand how someone who appeared zealous for godliness and fruitfulness could have such a marriage. No one seems to deny that Wesley's marriage was disastrous and a blight on his record. His many biographers have described his marriage as "one of the greatest blunders he ever made,"[10] "a preposterous union,"[11] "a martyrdom that lasted thirty years,"[12] "the fatal mistake,"[13] "a severe trial,"[14] "the worst mistake of John's life,"[15] and a "thirty years' war with Molly."[16] One biographer described Wesley's wedding day by saying, "It is pretty certain that no loves lighted their torches on this occasion."[17] Another biographer summed it all up when he lamented, "Had he searched the whole kingdom, he would hardly have found a woman more unsuitable in these respects, than she whom he married."[18]

Such a pathetic situation raises many questions. Most of Wesley's biographers, especially the earlier ones, lay sole blame on Mrs. Wesley. Current writings suggest Wesley bore some responsibility as well. This latter view is the conclusion I have come to as well. An analysis of Wesley's Biblical and theological convictions regarding how he viewed his role as a husband and father as well as being a minister of the gospel sheds much light on how and why this disastrous marriage occurred. Hopefully, we can learn from this in our own day in order to encourage our ministers, church leaders, missionaries, and lay people to be blameless, above reproach, and have a good conscience so that Christ may be honored in all that we say and do.

Wesley's Convictions Regarding the Role of a Husband and Father

An examination of Wesley's views regarding the role of a husband and father reveal that Wesley believed that a husband and father had certain Biblical responsibilities to his wife and children. Regarding the role of a husband, in his sermon entitled, "On Family Religion," he taught husbands,

> The person in your house that claims your first and nearest attention, is, undoubtedly your wife; seeing you are to love her, even as Christ hath loved the Church, when he laid down his life for it, that he might 'purify it unto himself, not having spot or wrinkle or any such thing.' The same end is every husband to pursue, in all his intercourse with his wife; to use every possible means that she may be freed from every spot, and may walk unblamable in love.[19]

It is interesting to note that the above quote was written in 1783, two years after his wife's death, and after thirty years of marriage. This was his settled conviction written later in life, not just youthful idealism. One wonders if he believed he fulfilled this in his marriage?

Elsewhere in a sermon entitled "The Duties of Husbands and Wives" he exhorted his hearers that,

> the wife is to have the highest place in the husband's heart, and he in her's. No neighbour, no friend, no parent, no child, should be so near and dear to either as the other ... They must do more, and suffer more for each other, than any other in all the world ... the

husband must do or leave undone, any thing he can, that he may please his wife ... in diet, attire, choice of company, and all things else, each must fulfill the other's desire as absolutely as can be done, without transgressing the law of God ... helpful fidelity consists in their mutual care to abstain from and prevent whatever might grieve or hurt either.[20]

Wesley preached a lofty picture of the husband's role in the marriage relationship. Not only did he teach that the wife was to have first place in her husband's heart over all other persons, but that the husband was to do whatever he could to please his wife. This would extend to what he ate, what he wore, who he chose as his company, and in fact, to all things. The husband, taught Wesley, was to do whatever it took to please his wife and to keep from hurting her. In commenting on Ephesians 5:25, "even as Christ also loved the Church," he wrote, "Here is the true model of conjugal affection. With this kind of affection, with this degree of it, and to this end should husbands love their wives."[21] It would seem that if Wesley followed his own teaching he would have made a caring and devoted husband, who would do whatever he could to please his wife as long as it did not conflict with God's Word.

Wesley also preached on the father's role. In the above sermon, "On Family Religion," he said to fathers,

Next to your wife are your children; immortal spirits whom God hath, for a time, entrusted to your care, that you may train them up in all holiness, and fit them for the enjoyment of God in eternity. This is a glorious and important trust; seeing one soul is of more value than all the world beside. Every child, therefore, you are to watch over with the utmost care, that, when you are called to give an account of each to the Father of Spirits, you may give your accounts with joy and not with grief.[22]

Fathers are not to "part with them while they are young; it being your duty to "train them up," with all care, "in the way wherein they should go.""[23] Fathers should "particularly endeavour to instruct" their children "early, plainly, *frequently*, and patiently."[24] He continued,

> It would be of little service to do it only once or twice a week. How often do you feed their bodies? Not less than three times a day. And is the soul of less value than the body? Will you not then feed this as often?[25]

Wesley believed fathers were to be devoted to their children's spiritual well-being, spending much time instructing them in the ways of the Lord. Family prayer was to be a daily occurrence. No opportunity should be lost to instruct one's children in the ways of the Lord.

Wesley's Convictions Regarding the Role of a Minister of the Gospel

Of course, the question arises as to whether Wesley lived out his own teachings. As one examines his relationship with his wife, there seems to be some disparity between what he instructed and what he actually did, especially in his choice of company. There also seems to be disparity in his statements regarding the role of a father. It is uncertain how young Molly's children were when John married her.[26] Noah, her youngest, may have been only four years old. If they were young, he was clearly inconsistent with what he preached, because he frequently left them when they were young due to ministry travels. We also know that earlier when he almost married another woman Wesley said that any children they would have had were to be brought up at Kingswood, the orphanage he founded. This would allow him to continue his itinerant ministry.[27] Granted, this woman was the headmistress of the orphanage, but that still leaves him itinerating while his children were small. If, as stated earlier, he said fathers are not to part with their children while they are young, but are to "train them up" and teach them frequently, how can he justify his expansive ministry travels?

His perspective regarding children also comes out in his response to his brother Charles when Charles began to slow down his travels as a minister in order to be home with his family. John felt Charles was too preoccupied with family matters and needed to be itinerating again. In an ironic statement (in light of his own troubled marriage) he exhorted Charles, "We must be all devoted to God. Then wives, sons, daughters will be blessings. Eia age; rumpe moras! (Come on, act; break off delay!)" [Feb. 28, 1766].[28]

All this seems hard to square with John Wesley's preaching regarding the role of a husband and father. How could Wesley reconcile what appears to be contradictory views? The answer lies in Wesley's conviction that the "work of the Lord" (i.e. the Methodist cause) was synonymous with commitment to God. Thus, "the cause" was a higher priority than marriage and family. When John wrote to his brother and exhorted him to be "all devoted to God," he meant to the cause (i.e. the Methodist cause). This entailed an unswerving commitment to an itinerant ministry. Itinerancy was crucial in John Wesley's thinking. He believed that if ministers settled in one place, both the people and the minister would get bored. Six to eight weeks was long enough in one place or all would grow cold. John assumed that Charles could not be totally devoted to God unless he put the Methodist cause first and began to itinerate again. John wanted to "spend and be spent in the work" of itinerancy and he wanted Charles to do the same. But Charles' conviction was that marriage and family are also "God's cause." Therefore Charles' decision to be home did not mitigate either his devotion to God or his honoring God in his choice. Though some have felt this decision "maimed" Charles' ministry,[29] it is significant to note that when Charles made the transition to be home more, his ministry focus shifted from itinerant preaching to the writing of hymns. Hardly anyone would dispute the rich legacy he left to the church through his hymns. Not only did his hymns enrich the worship of the church, but much deep theology was, and still is, taught to believers. What a great loss to the Body of Christ if Charles had not slowed down his travels!

Because many men and women have been used greatly by God while neglecting their families, neglect of one's family has often been justified. This type of pragmatic thinking doesn't prove anything. What we do not know is whether someone's fruitfulness could be greater and more far reaching if one was devoted to *both* family and ministry. The legacy of Charles Wesley through his hymns is a powerful reminder that God does not need us to sacrifice our families to get His work done.

Wesley's beliefs are seen elsewhere as well. In a sermon on "Spiritual Idolatry," Wesley said that we must be careful not to idolize those in our family. He said,

> Let this be carefully considered, even by those who [sic] God has joined together; by husbands and wives, parents and children. It cannot be denied, that these ought to love one another tenderly. They are commanded so to do. But they are neither commanded nor permitted to love one another idolatrously. Yet how common is this! How frequently is a husband, a wife, a child, put in the place of God. How many that are accounted good Christians fix their affections on each other, so as to leave no place for God! They seek their happiness in the creature, not the Creator. One may truly say to the other, "I view thee, lord and end of my desires." That is, "I desire nothing more but thee! Thou art the thing that I long for! All my desire is unto thee, and unto the remembrance of thy name." Now if this is not flat idolatry, I cannot tell what is.[30]

The Scriptures make it clear that if any thing, including another person, comes before God in a person's affections or loyalty, this is idolatry. The question is whether commitment to a cause, such as the Methodist cause (or perhaps even one's own public ministry), is to be solely equated with commitment to God. If it is, then it is idolatry not to put the cause (or one's public ministry) before one's family. This was John Wesley's conviction. However, is family just a subordinate "cause," or is it God's cause and thus worthy of an equally ardent fervor to give oneself? This seemed to be Charles' perspective. But for John Wesley, it was the Methodist cause that captured his heart. He made this very clear to his wife when he wrote, "everything which is in my power I do and will do to oblige you; everything you desire, unless I judge it would hurt my own soul, or yours, or *the cause of God*" [July 12, 1760].[31] To this cause alone John Wesley desired to "spend and be spent in the work" [May 28, 1753].[32]

Wesley's belief that the Methodist cause was a higher priority than marriage extended to whether a person should even marry. His perspective was that singleness was a better state in which to accomplish the Lord's work and therefore one should remain single if at all possible. In 1743, he published a tract entitled "Thoughts on a Single Life." In it he said that to forbid marriage was the "doctrine of devils." Since "perfection" consisted in one's entire devotion to God, not ultimately one's marital state, neither marriage nor singleness was the more perfect state. And certainly it is better to marry than to burn with passion. However, those "happy few" who could remain single for "the sake of the kingdom of heaven" should do so. Singleness, said Wesley, has many advantages over marriage. One can live entirely for God's glory and never have to worry about pleasing anyone else but God. One also doesn't have to worry about getting "entangled" by loving someone above God. All one's time, talents, and treasures can be given to God without having to see if it is agreeable with one's wife. For example, a single man can give all his time to God without having to ask his wife if he can do something ("otherwise what complaints or disgust would follow" on her part). One also doesn't have to worry about any of the thousands of domestic trials and sorrows with which fathers get "entangled," such as "sick, weak, unhappy, or disobedient children." Keep away from such "foolish desires," counselled Wesley, and avoid all needless conversations with women so that you are not tempted to "cast away" this gift of singleness.[33]

Wesley's views never changed on this. Four days after he decided to marry Molly (Feb. 6, 1751), he spoke to a group of single men and encouraged them to remain single, "unless a particular case might be the exception to the general rule."[34] Twenty years later, he recorded in his Journal his "present thoughts upon a single life, which indeed, are just the same they have been these thirty years" [Nov. 5, 1764].[35]

Looking at Wesley's teaching in the light of Scripture, it is clear that singleness is a gift with great advantages. One's interests are divided when married, while single men and women are free to pursue "undistracted devotion to the Lord" (I Cor. 7:35). However, Wesley goes beyond the Word of God when he calls marriage a "foolish desire." Paul in this same passage called marriage, as well as singleness, a gift.

One must also ask, if a wife and children are an entanglement? For example, does a husband spending time with his wife mean he is not free to give his time to God? Or is it possible that in spending time with his wife his time is being given to God? Perhaps such a use of his time glorifies God more fully by manifesting to a watching world Christ's intimate relationship with His Bride? And are weak and sick children an entanglement? Or could God in His sovereignty deem that such children are the means by which a godly father reflects the glory of the compassion and tenderness the LORD Himself has for the helpless? What may be an entanglement to Wesley may be an opportunity to God to bring great glory to Himself by choosing "the weak things of the world to shame the things which are strong" (I Cor. 1:27). Perhaps such a ministry in the life of a godly father glorifies God more fully by manifesting to a watching world the glory of the mercy of God. Of course the thought also crosses one's mind how someone could be so easily tempted to "cast away" such a gift if one is so happy. These and other questions need to be addressed.

If an itinerant preacher did marry, being totally devoted to the cause meant that marriage would not hinder an itinerant preacher's travel schedule at all. One month after his marriage Wesley wrote just that in his Journal, "I cannot understand how a Methodist preacher can answer it [sic] to God to preach one sermon or travel one day less in a married than in a single state. In this respect surely 'it remaineth that they who have wives be as though they had none'" [March 19, 1751].[36]

Wesley, after sixteen and a half years of marriage, counselled one of his preachers to tell his future wife that,

> I dare not settle in any one place: God has called me to be a travelling preacher. Are you willing to accept of me upon these terms? And can you engage never directly or indirectly to hinder me from travelling? If not, it is best for us to part [Sept. 2, 1767].[37]

How Wesley's Convictions Related to His Marriage

As far as we know, John Wesley lived this out regardless of his wife. Being newly married did not deter him. Right after he married, he continued to preach. Though his ankle injury did keep him initially from travelling, it did not stop him from preaching, on his knees of course![38]

Soon afterwards he resumed his travels. It was only one month after his marriage that he wrote in his journal that he would not preach one less sermon or travel one less mile just because he was married. This he continued throughout the rest of his marriage. Once when he heard his wife was "dangerously ill" he immediately left to see her. Upon arriving at 1:00 a.m., he found that "the fever was turned, and the danger over." An hour later he set out again. There was a conference two days later that he did not want to miss![39] As we shall see later, no matter what her trials, he did not slacken his pace to support her.

With such a perspective, one is perplexed why Wesley did "cast away" his gift of singleness. He once declared that his main objection to ever getting married was that "A Dispensation of the Gospel has been committed to me. And I will do nothing which directly or indirectly tends to hinder my preaching ye Gospel."[40] Why did he disregard his own convictions? Wesley received counsel from Vincent Perronet on this very issue and wrote in his Journal on February 2, 1751,

> after having received a full answer from Mr. Perronet, I was clearly convinced I ought to marry. For many years I remained single, because I believed I could be more useful in a single state than in a married state. And I praise God who enabled me so to do. I now as fully believed that in my present circumstances I might be more useful in a married state.[41]

We later learn in Charles' Journal why John felt he could be more useful. Less than two weeks after he married, John said that during a recent visit to "Oxford he had no more thought of a woman than for any other being; that he married to break down the prejudice about the world and him."[42] His new wife listened to this "open-eyed."[43] This indeed must have been surprising and hard news to hear.

The marriage to Molly Vazeille was not only hasty but John seemed to be on, what we would call, the rebound. In 1749, John had been engaged to another woman named Grace Murray.[44] She was committed to the cause of Methodism and might have made John an excellent wife. Grace Murray was a remarkable woman. Both her devotion to Christ and her zeal and fruitfulness in ministry made her one of the more significant female leaders in Methodism. Her responsibilities were extensive and included visiting the sick, a group leader, meeting with women, pioneering work, and traveling to meet with and organize the female societies.[45] Her energy level whether natural or fired by the Spirit of God enabled her to praise God til 4:00 in the morning and then still go from place to place without getting tired, as she herself claimed.[46] John Wesley described her as "inexpressibly tender"[47] and "eminently compassionate."[48] He said, "she had a measure which I never found in any other both Grace and Gifts and Fruit."[49] He also said she possessed "deep knowledge of the things of God"[50] and "many have been convinced of sin by her private conversation."[51] He said that she was everything he wanted in a woman; as a housekeeper, a nurse, a friend, a companion, and as a fellow laborer.[52] He spoke extremely highly of her and challenged others to "shew me ye Woman in England, Wales, or Ireland, who has already done so much good as Grace Murray. I will say no more. Shew me one in all ye English Annals, whom God has employed in so high a degree? I might say, in all ye history of the Church, from ye death of our Lord to this day ... This is no hyperbole, but plain, demonstrable fact."[53] It was no wonder that Wesley fell in love with her and desired to marry her so that she would then be his "fellow-labourer in ye Gospel."

Unfortunately, Charles was against the marriage and even had a part in marrying her off to another man behind John's back.[54] It seems that the intended marriage was causing problems in the movement. It was even thought that the entire Methodist movement was in jeopardy over this marriage. Charles claimed, "All our Preachers would leave us, all our Societies disperse,"[55] and the marriage would "put a stop to ye whole work of GOD."[56] There are a number of reasons why Charles was against the marriage. First, Charles knew how marriage would hinder John's ministry and thus believed John should stay single. Second, Grace was a domestic servant. In the eighteenth century most marriages were usually within one's own social class. Charles felt Grace's station was too low for John.[57] But the main reason is that Charles thought Grace was engaged to another man and this would bring scandal on the Methodist cause if John Wesley married her.[58] Two men, John Wesley and John Bennet, wanted to marry Grace. She could not decide which one she wanted to marry and at different times agreed to marry each one of them. In fact, she supposedly entered into a contract with each one of them called a depraesenti contract, which was legally binding in English law.[59] No one knows who she contracted with first and both men claimed they had the prior claim. Charles Wesley believed it was John Bennet to whom she belonged and he convinced Grace Murray that if she did not marry John Bennet the consequences would be disastrous for both her and the Methodist cause. With Charles' influence and help, Grace and Bennet were married behind John Wesley's back. Wesley was heartbroken, and still claimed Grace was rightfully his wife both legally and morally. [60] George Whitefield believed Grace belonged to John Wesley and that Charles' "impetuosity prevailed and bore down all before it."[61] After Grace's wedding,

Charles and his brother talked. Charles realized his brother was innocent and Grace did belong to him. Charles then blamed Grace for vacillating between the two men.[62] Wesley was heartbroken. He had believed that God had prepared Grace to be his wife. He had spent time with her observing her character and commitment to Methodism.[63] If there was any criticism of her, he spoke with those individuals to see if there was any substance to their criticism.[64] Being satisfied that she was above reproach, he proceeded with the relationship.[65] Now Grace was married to another man.[66] He wrote thirty-one verses to describe his heartache which give us a deeper insight into the man. He asked God why He brought her to him, only to take her away. Although he was unable to understand God's plan and though his heart was bleeding, he would submit to the Lord's will and God would be his Love, his Joy, his eternal portion.[67] He continued to minister as before and wrote, "If I had had more regard for her I loved, than for the Work of God, I would have gone straight to Newcastle ... I knew this was giving up all: But I knew GOD called."[68] In other words, though God was his love, his joy, his eternal portion, it was the work of God which was first in his thoughts. No woman would ever come before the "work of God."

This was the background to John Wesley's hasty and impetuous marriage to Molly Vazeille. He was determined to marry. When Mrs. Vazeille came into the picture, he seized the opportunity. When Charles found out that John was determined to marry, he wrote in his Journal,

> I was thunderstruck, and could only answer, he had
> given me the first blow, and his marriage would come
> like the *coup de grace*. Trusty Ned Perronet followed,
> and told me, the person was Mrs. Vazeille! one of
> whom I had never had the least suspicion. I refused
> his company to the chapel, and retired to mourn with
> my faithful Sally. I groaned all the day, and several
> following ones, under my own and the people's
> burden. I could eat no pleasant food, nor preach, nor
> rest, either by night or by day [Feb. 2, 1751].[69]

Many theories have been advanced as to why
Charles was so upset. The most logical reason seems
to be that upon John's return from Georgia the
brothers promised each other that neither would marry
or even take a step towards it without the knowledge
and consent of the other.[70] This accountability was to
be a safeguard against the temptation of marrying the
wrong person. Charles had fulfilled this commitment
when he married Sally.[71] John, fearful that Charles
would interfere as he did previously, told Charles of
his intended marriage but did not seek his consent.[72]
He thus broke his commitment, causing a temporary
strain in their relationship. If John had fulfilled his
obligation to his brother and sought his consent, it is
possible he would not have married Mrs. Vazeille. Not
only did he violate his conviction to seek his brother's
approval, but he also violated his conviction not to
marry someone before he could clearly determine the
character of the intended woman. As stated previously,
in the case of Grace Murray, he had carefully observed
her over time, even to the point of questioning any
who had a problem with her. But when it came to

Molly Vazeille, he did not do this. He had earlier insisted, "If ever I have a wife, she ought to be the most usefull Woman in ye kingdom: Not barely one, who probably *may* be so, (I could not be content to run such a hazard) but one that undeniably is so."[73]

Sadly, he learned by his own experience the truth of his own commentary on Proverbs 30:23. John's reason why the earth cannot bear up when an unloved woman gets married is because then "she displays all those ill humors which before she concealed."[74] Henry Moore, close friend and biographer, himself said she had given the appearance of being "truly pious" and "very agreeable in her person and manners." But, he added, "she departed, however, from this excellent way."[75] Perhaps if he had waited and observed her more carefully, he would have realized she had neither the character nor the commitment to ministry he had. John later acknowledged his marriage had been hasty.[76] As William Shakespeare said, "Hasty marriage seldom proveth well."

Wesley was unreservedly committed to ministry. Unfortunately, he married a woman who was not committed to ministry in the same way. As stated previously, he was resolved never to slacken his labours. He also believed it was his wife's duty to obey. In his attempt to "fulfill his calling," Molly was either to travel with him or be content with an absent husband.[77] To her credit, Molly did try and initially travelled with him until the fall of 1755. But this proved to be a hard life for her. One can hardly blame her. She was a middle-aged woman and the hardships were many. They frequently met with harsh climate conditions which never deterred Wesley. Oftentimes there were violent wind or rain storms. One time, while he was preaching, a violent storm blew down the house opposite from where they were. While the storm continued and as Wesley described, "the tiles of the houses around them were rattling," they (he, his wife, and her daughter) set out for the next destination. Fortunately they arrived safely.[78] Situations like this were common, creating poor road conditions and danger to travellers, but the itinerants were not stopped. Travels by sea were no easier. Storms created rough seas which caused extreme seasickness among passengers, Mrs. Wesley included.[79] Through all the hardships, Wesley wrote to his friend Ebenezer Blackwell regarding his wife's response, "After taking a round of between three and four hundred miles, we came hither yesterday in the afternoon. My wife is at least as well as when we left London: the more she travels the better she bears it ... I was at first a little afraid she would not so well understand the behavior of a Yorkshire mob; but there has been no trial" [April 16, 1752].[80]

He spoke too soon. Eight days later a mob acting as though they were "possessed by Moloch" threw "stones and clods" at them. A woman invited them into her carriage. The mob continued to throw whatever they could into the windows. A large gentlewoman sat on Wesley and screened him so that he was safe. We don't know whether Mrs. Wesley received the same protection![81] This was not the only situation involving mobs. They were frequent enough that Wesley commented, "now we can even walk unmolested."[82]

Also, during these travels, she was often separated from her children. Friends cared for them while she travelled with John.[83] At one point, she received word that one of her sons was dying. She left to pay her last respects to her son alone! Fortunately, she made it in time to see him before he died.[84]

Living conditions were not always pleasant on these journeys. Molly was not content and often expressed this to John. He felt her "fretting" was a greater burden. After she discontinued her travels with him, he wrote to his friend Ebenezer Blackwell and compared his current situation with when she was with him. He wrote,

> In my last journey into the North, all my patience was put to the proof again and again, and all my endeavours to please, yet without success. In my present journey I leap, as broke from chains. I am content with whatever entertainment I meet with, and my companions are always in good humour 'because they are with me.' This must be the spirit of all who take journeys with me. If a dinner ill dressed, or hard bed, a poor room, a shower of rain, or a dusty road will put them out of humour, it lays a burden upon me greater than all the rest put together. By the grace of God I never fret; I repine at nothing; I am discontented with nothing. And to have persons fretting and murmuring at everything is like tearing the flesh off my bones. I see God sitting upon His throne and ruling all things well [Aug. 31, 1755].[85]

Though one must admire such faith on Wesley's part, it is also difficult not to have compassion for a middle-aged woman who struggled with such hardships.

Molly stopped travelling with John in 1755. From that point on she rarely saw him. Even when he was back in London and claimed to "rest," he kept quite busy. In one such day of rest he expounded seven chapters and preached six sermons![86] John knew she had many trials yet he never slackened his pace to support her. Her difficulties were not slight either. John himself tells us what they were. He said that God "has given you a dutiful but sickly daughter; He has taken away one of your sons. Another has been a grievous cross; as the third will probably be. He has suffered you to be defrauded of much money; He has chastened you with strong pain" [July 15, 1774].[87] He did not demonstrate compassion when he said that these were the means that God had used to "curb your stubborn will and break the impetuosity of your temper."[88]

His relationships with other women also caused many problems in their marriage. John Wesley corresponded extensively with many women all for "the cause." Initially he told Molly that in his absence she could open any letters directed to him.[89] Her jealous response to some of the letters from other women caused him to regret this and he began to direct his mail to others. She found out about this and became more suspicious and jealous. Now that "all the intrigue is discovered," this "raised a violent storm." [90] Early on in their marriage we see her insecurity. In his MS journal he wrote in shorthand,

[My wife, upon a] supposition that [I did not love her, and that I trusted others more than her, had] often fretted herself almost to death. I was always enabled to accept it at God's hands, and calmly to say, Why doth a living man complain? Nevertheless I determined to use all means; and today I explained with her at large. By the blessing of God the cloud vanished away, and we were united as at the beginning [Dec. 16, 1751].[91]

The letters he wrote to other women do contain affectionate language.[92] For example, to Dorothy Furly he wrote, "Write as often and as freely and fully as you please."[93] To Mrs. Abigail Brown he wrote, "Speak freely to me, if you love me."[94] To Ann Foard he wrote, "how is it that you make me write longer letters to you than I do almost to any one else?"[95] To Peggy Dale he wrote, "I thought it hardly possible for me to love you better than I did before I came last to Newcastle. But your artless, simple, undisguised affection exceedingly increased mine. At the same time it increased my confidence in you, so that I feel you are unspeakably near and dear to me."[96] To Ann (Nancy) Bolton he wrote, "O Nancy, I want sadly to see you ... I want to know everything that concerns you ... Your last visit endeared you to me exceedingly ... Don't think of sending me anything; your love is sufficient."[97]

The woman who seemed to cause the most problems was Sarah Ryan.[98] She had a disreputable past. She had been a domestic servant who married a man she did not know was already married. She then became engaged to an Italian only to fall for and marry a seafaring Irishman named Ryan. At one point it appeared that Ryan was lost at sea, so she went back to the Italian. When Ryan came back, he called her back only to abandon her.[99] She then became a Methodist, and was appointed by Wesley to be the housekeeper at Kingswood.[100] His correspondence to her was quite affectionate. He wrote, "I can hardly avoid trembling for you still: upon what a pinnacle do you stand."[101] Even worse, he was vulnerable with her and confided in her regarding his marital difficulties. In one letter he shared his feelings regarding Molly's treatment of him. He wrote,

> Your last letter was seasonable indeed. I was growing faint in my mind. The being watched over for evil; the having every word I spoke, every action I did (small and great) watched over with no friendly eye; the hearing a thousand little, tart, unkind reflections in return for the kindest words I could devise, – Like drops of eating water on the marble, At length have worn my sinking spirits down. Yet I could not say, 'Take Thy plague away from me,' but only, 'Let me be purified, not consumed' [Feb. 10, 1758].[102]

Wesley did question whether he should continue to write to Sarah after his wife threatened to leave him, but after he prayed about it, he decided he should continue the correspondence. One biographer says of the letter Wesley wrote regarding this situation, we "regret his writing such a letter, on such a subject, to such a woman. His motives and his end were unquestionably pure; but the act itself cannot be defended. His wife was jealous, cruelly jealous, and he ought to have avoided what was likely to feed and increase her passion."[103]

Molly Wesley's fears may not have been unfounded. Wesley later wrote to Sarah Ryan and said, "It has frequently been said, and with some appearance of truth, that you endeavour to monopolize the affections of all that fall into your hands; that you destroy the nearest and dearest connexion they had before, and make them quite cool and indifferent to their most intimate friends. I do not speak at all on my own account; I set myself out of the question. But if there be anything of the kind with regard to other people, I should be sorry both for them and you."[104] Tyerman, a well-known eighteenth century biographer of Wesley said, "No one, for instance, will for a moment attempt to justify his writing, in the terms just quoted, to Sarah Ryan, his Bristol housekeeper, who, however pious after her conversion, lived a most disreputable life before it. This was, to say the least, supremely foolish." However he does add, "but still it was not sufficient to justify his wife's subsequent cruel and insane behavior."[105] Later, we will comment on his wife's response.

I have to agree with Tyerman. It was foolish. First of all, a comparison of Wesley's letters to women with those of George Whitefield (as we shall see later) reveal that such free and affectionate language was not necessary. Whitefield also corresponded with many women yet his language demonstrated a deep commitment without such forward and affectionate language. Second, it is clear that it was Wesley's correspondence as well as his relationships with other women that provoked his wife's jealousy. She accused him of adultery and used the letters he wrote to other women as evidence.

This was not only foolish, but Wesley had to be either incredibly naïve about women, enjoyed them too much to care, believed his ministry to them was too significant, or some combination of the above. Wesley enjoyed the company of women and felt comfortable with them. He said of his Oxford years that he questioned whether he "loved woman or company more than God?"[106] His sister Hetty told him that he liked "woman merely for being woman."[107] During his mission trip to Georgia, John wrote to Charles, "I stand in jeopardy every hour. Two or three are women, younger, refined, God-fearing," and then he added, "Pray that I know none of them after the flesh."[108] It is true, this was before his conversion, but even after his conversion, this enjoyment of the female sex persisted. A Moravian named James Hutton wrote in his memoirs under the date of March 14th, 1740, "Both John and Charles Wesley are dangerous snares to many young women. Several are in love with them. I wish they were married to some good sisters, though I would not give them one of mine, even if I had many…".[109]

Wesley's magnetic personality coupled with his leadership of the Methodist movement caused many women to be enamored with him. One anecdote illustrates this. When he went to Bath he went into a house and was told by the maid that a group of women were wanting to speak to him. When he entered the room "the ladies gazed upon him as if he were a supernatural being." He said, "Ladies, I believe the maid was mistaken; she said you desired to speak with me, but you only wanted to look at me."[110] I do not want to spend too much time on the charm of John Wesley, but suffice it to say that his warm and affectionate manner with women coupled with his position of leadership in Methodism would naturally draw the attention of women. It would be naïve of any man not to realize how women would respond to him. He claimed he had no sensual desires for these women and that he was completely pure. His sincerity is not in question. It is his discernment that is questioned. Charles, it was said, was discerning of people's character,[111] but he said that John was "born for the benefit of knaves."[112] John's trusting and naïve nature led to foolish behavior. It even opened the door to false accusations in regard to his moral purity with women.[113] A less godly man would not have been able to resist the power of sensual desire and ego gratification. Even so, to avoid the appearance of evil is a good caveat for any individual in spiritual leadership. It must also be stated that it is the rare wife, if she even exists, who would not be threatened by this. Even Grace Murray, who was both godly and committed to ministry, struggled with jealousy over Wesley's attention to another woman.[114]

Wesley did stop writing to Sarah for a while and his wife seemed to be better. However, because the change was only temporary,[115] he believed it did no good and began to insist on his "right" to write and converse with whomever he pleased. Wesley believed it was up to his conscience and she was to accept that.[116] He told her that he had "the same right to claim obedience"[117] from her as she had from her son.[118] To Blackwell he wrote, "I certainly will, as long as I can hold a pen, assert my right of conversing with whom I please. Reconciliation or none, let *her* look to that. If the unbeliever will depart, let her depart [July 12, 1758].[119] This was a primary "bone of contention" throughout their married life. She accused him of "unkindness, cruelty, and what not" for insisting on choosing his own company (i.e. women). He insisted on holding to his "right," and stated, "I will not, I cannot, I dare not give it up."[120]

This insistence on his "right" is very difficult to square with his teaching that we quoted earlier that a husband should do whatever he could to please his wife, even in his choice of company. Not to mention that Wesley earlier acknowledged in his relationship with Grace Murray that if he had married her, "she would remove many hindrances from others, from women in particular ... because I should converse far more sparingly with them. Perhaps not in private with any young women at all..."[121] This had to be an incredible blindspot. Perhaps Wesley felt he was somehow above his own teaching. Perhaps Wesley would respond the same way he responded when asked about the legitimacy of women preaching. He wrote to one such woman preacher, "I think the strength of the cause rests there, on your having an extraordinary call. So, I am persuaded has every (sic) our lay-preachers. Otherwise I could not countenance this preaching at all. It is plain to me, that the whole work of God called Methodism is an extraordinary dispensation of His Providence. Therefore I do not wonder, if several things occur therein which do not fall under ordinary Rules of Discipline..."[122] Perhaps he believed his unique call at such a unique time in history superseded "ordinary Rules of Discipline" and included encouraging the ladies even at the expense of his wife.

Her Response to His Convictions

Although life was difficult being married to a man who saw "the world as his parish," Molly Wesley's reaction did not help. It was her reaction that caused Wesley's earlier biographers to lay sole blame on her. Southey said, "But, of all women, she is said to have been the most unsuited to him. Fain would she have made him, like Marc Antony, give up all for love; and being disappointed in that hope, she tormented him in such a manner, by her outrageous jealousy, and abominable temper, that she deserves to be classed in a triad with Xantippe and the wife of Job, as one of the three bad wives."[123] Telford said, "The stone erected over her grave in Camberwell churchyard described her as "a woman of exemplary piety, a tender parent, and a sincere friend." Whatever she may have been in these respects, she was one of the worst wives of whom we have ever read. She darkened thirty years of Wesley's life by her intolerable jealousy, her malicious and violent temper. Wesley would never sacrifice his duty to personal feeling, but though he was a roving husband, a more tender or pleasant companion no woman could desire."[124] Tyerman said, "As a rule, she was a bitter unmitigated curse," and called her a "twitting wife."[125] The Vicar of Everton called her "a ferret."[126] And others would concur that "the most charitable view of Mrs. Wesley's conduct is that she suffered from some mental unsoundness."[127] They certainly did not think highly of this woman!

It is true, Molly Wesley had an extremely strong temper, fueled by jealousy.[128] This led to bitterness which was followed by deliberate and vindictive actions against her husband. Besides getting angry at him, she tried to hurt him. For example, to irk him, though there were five rooms in the house, she disassembled a bed and put it in his study, his only room in the house.[129]

Throughout their entire married life she accused him of adultery with many different women.[130] One biographer charged that Mrs. Wesley went so far as to accuse even Charles' wife, Sally, of being John's mistress. "Charles danced with rage at this imputation."[131]

Wesley claimed that she also constantly spoke evil of him to others behind his back, claiming things that were not true, such as he beat her,[132] or he never wrote to her but he wrote to other women.[133] He said that she threw "squibs" at him in public.[134] He also claimed that she lied to others about his words to her. In one such incident, he said that when he arrived at Limerick, he spoke to Thomas Walsh. Walsh asked him, "'How did you part with Mrs. Wesley the last time?' On my (Wesley's) saying, 'Very affectionately,' he replied, 'Why, what a woman is this! She told me your parting words were, 'I hope to see your wicked face no more.'"[135]

Molly picked John Wesley's lock and stole some of his letters and papers.[136] Then she showed them to others to mar his character.[137] She even gave them to his enemies to have them published.[138] Wesley said to her, "You have published my (real and supposed) faults, not to one or two intimates only (though perhaps that would have been too much), but to all Bristol, to all London, to all England, to all Ireland. Yea, you did whatever in you lay to publish it to all the world, thereby designing to put a sword into my enemies' hands."[139]

Charles' daughter, in a letter to a friend just before her death, claimed Mrs. Wesley even forged some of John's letters for publication. She wrote,

> I think it was in the year 1775 ... Mrs. Wesley had obtained some letters which she used to the most injurious purposes, misinterpreting spiritual expressions, and interpolating words. These she read to some Calvinists, and they were to be sent to the Morning Post. A Calvinist gentleman, who esteemed my uncle, came to the former, and told him that, for the sake of religion, the publication should be stopped, and Mr. John Wesley be allowed to answer for himself. As Mrs. Wesley had read, but did not show, the letters to him, he had some doubts of their authenticity; and though they were addressed to Mr. John Wesley, they might be forgeries; at any rate he ought not to leave town at such a juncture, but clear the matter satisfactorily. My dear father, to whom the reputation of my uncle was far dearer than his own, immediately saw the importance of refutation, and set off to the Foundery to induce him to postpone his journey ... Never shall I forget the manner in which my father accosted my mother on his return home. 'My brother,' says he, 'is indeed an

extraordinary man. I placed before him the importance of the character of a minister; the evil consequences which might result from his indifference ... His reply was, Brother, when I devoted to God my ease, my time, my life, did I except my reputation? No. Tell Sally I will take her to Canterbury tomorrow.' I ought to add, that the letters in question were satisfactorily proved to be mutilated, and no scandal resulted from his trust in God.[140]

Many of his followers circulated stories concerning Molly's treatment of John. John Hampson, one of Wesley's preachers, claimed that he walked into a room and found Mrs. Wesley furious. John was "on the floor, where she had been trailing him by the hair of his head; and she herself was still holding in her hand the venerable locks which she had plucked up by the roots."[141] Another story alleges that she frequently drove a hundred miles in her carriage to spy on him. She wanted to see with whom he came into town.[142] If the above stories are true, they lend further evidence that Mrs. Wesley's anger led her to strong vindictive measures.

If her anger were reserved for her husband alone, then we could assume it was due to John's faults. However, she was bitter towards others as well. For example, she seemed to be bitter towards anyone who defended his character (such as one Clayton Carthy).[143] In two separate letters to his wife, Charles spoke of others who struggled with Mrs. Wesley. He wrote, "Poor Mr. Lefevre breakfasted with me this morning, and lamented that he cannot love her"[144] and "Miss

Norton is very much at your service; but flies before the face of my sister."[145] The Methodist people did not like Molly Wesley. John wrote to his wife, "If it were possible for you to observe one thing, 'Commit your cause unto the Lord, and speak nothing against me behind my back,' the people will love you. Till then they cannot."[146]

Molly Wesley treated others with scorn as well. Her servants were belittled by her (or to use Wesley's words – "browbeated, harassed, rated like dogs"), much to John's chagrin.[147] And of course, Sarah Ryan, another victim of her biting tongue, was berated for her past. For example, it was said that Mrs. Wesley walked into a room of people where both John and Sarah were eating and announced, "The whore now serving you has three husbands living."[148]

But above all, Mrs. Wesley quarreled with Charles and his wife Sally. The quarrel lasted about seven years and began early in John's marriage.[149] Three years after he was married, John thought he was dying from consumption. His last request was for his wife and Charles to be reconciled. Both said they would, but it was short lived.[150] The quarrels were constant. Charles wrote with astonishment, "I called two minutes before preaching on Mrs. W-, at the Foundery; and in all that time had not one quarrel."[151] At one point, John even wondered if Charles would ever speak to her again.[152] Struggling to love Molly, Charles wrote to his wife and asked,

What shall you and I do to love her better? "Love your enemies" is with man impossible: but is anything too hard for God? I fear you do not *constantly* pray for her. I *must* pray, or sink into the spirit of revenge [April 29, 1755].[153]

Charles called her his "best friend" because she told him all his faults! During one such confrontation she took both John and Charles in a room, shut the door, and proceeded to tell them both their faults. Charles, in an effort to get away, began to recite Latin until she let them go![154] Mrs. Wesley often spoke of Charles' faults to John until John said he could no longer listen to her speak that way about his brother.[155] Charles warned his wife, "My brother and sister will call on you, I presume, next Wednesday. She continues quite placid and tame. You can be courteous without trusting her."[156] Even Charles acknowledged John's trials, "I do not wonder that my poor brother trembles and quakes at the thought of coming to London."[157]

Furthermore, in John Wesley's defense, Henry Moore, close friend and biographer, claimed that Mrs. Wesley agreed before they were married that he could continue his ministry as before. "He (John Wesley) has more than once mentioned to me, that it was agreed between him and Mrs. Wesley, previous to their marriage, that he should not preach one sermon, or travel one mile the less on that account. 'If I thought I should,' said he, 'my dear, as well as I love you, I would never see your face more.'"[158] In further defence of John, he wrote to her and told her that nothing would make him happier than if she would always be with him, provided she would have a good attitude and not talk about him behind his back. He wanted to minister with her and he wanted to see her lead a fruitful life, but her bitterness was too great.[159] In further defense of John Wesley, he wrote to his wife many times and told her it was not too late. He would forgive her. Even as late as July 1774 he wrote,

> it might be an unspeakable blessing that you have a husband who knows your temper and can bear with it; who, after you have tried him numberless ways, laid to his charge things that he knew not, robbed him, betrayed his confidence, revealed his secrets, given him a thousand treacherous wounds, purposely aspersed and murdered his character, and made it your business so to do, under the pretense of vindicating your own character ... who, I say, after all these provocations, is still willing to forgive you at all ... As of yet the breach may be repaired; you have wronged me much, but not beyond forgiveness. I love you still [July 15, 1774].[160]

Three years later he began to insist on a retraction. He believed if he didn't his enemies would believe the lies were true.[161] Again, the cause influenced his action, but in this case it is hard not to pity the man.

Concluding Remarks

John Wesley, as history shows, was an incredibly influential man during the Revival. He was unequivocally committed to "spending and being spent" in the Methodist cause. For his zeal, his fruitfulness, and his commitment to seeing people come to Christ and mature, Wesley must be given due respect. His commitment to Christ, however, was inextricably linked to his commitment to the

Methodist cause. Marriage was valuable only if it enhanced his ministry. Even his motive and reasons to marry were all for the cause. He claimed he truly desired to love his wife and please her as long as it did not interfere with his call to ministry. Thus, he consistently put the needs of his public ministry ahead of the needs of his wife. He would not lessen his schedule just because he was married. It was his firm conviction that if he slackened at all, he would be disobedient to the work God had called him to do.

Even if Molly Wesley could have accepted this, she would never accept his relationships with other women. The conclusion I have come to is that it is probable if he had quit writing and interacting so closely with women, the problems in his marriage would have been considerably lessened. At the very least, she could not have accused him of adultery. However, he would not do this. Though she claimed it was unkind, even cruel, to do this, he insisted it was his "right" and she would have to accept this. He claimed it made no difference in her behavior when he stopped corresponding with Sarah Ryan, so he clung to his "right" to converse with and write to whoever he wanted.

In short, Wesley's commitment to Christ was synonymous with his public ministry. Wesley's perspective on his marriage was best summed up by Henry Moore, "He repeatedly told me, that he believed the LORD over-ruled this whole painful business for his good; and that if Mrs. Wesley had been a better wife, and had continued to act in that way in which she knew well how to act, he might have been unfaithful in the great work to which the LORD had called him, and might have too much sought to please her according to her own views."[162] In other words, Molly did alienate him, but he's grateful because it did not hinder the work of his ministry. If she had been a better wife, he might have been unfaithful to God's call on his life. The cause of Methodism was John Wesley's all consuming passion. The cause of Methodism had preeminence in his heart.

Molly Wesley, on the other hand, was a jealous and angry woman, perhaps even mentally unsound. She became bitter and maliciously tried to make his life difficult. Her response to her husband further alienated him.[163] She quarreled with many others as well. Their marriage was disastrous and she died a bitter old woman.

After that fateful day in 1771 when Molly left John, he did not recall her but she did return to him only to leave him again.[164] This time the breach was irreparable. On September 1, 1777, he said he sincerely wished a reunion and would take her back on three conditions, one of which was to retract her accusations against him (such as adultery).[165] She apparently would not retract. On October 2, 1778, he wrote what was perhaps his last letter to her, "As it is doubtful, considering your age and mine, whether we may meet anymore in this world, I think it right to tell you my mind once for all without either anger or bitterness ... If you were to live a thousand years, you could not undo the mischief you have done. And till you have done all you can towards it, I bid you farewell."[166]

There was no reconciliation after this. When his

son-in-law, who was married to Molly's daughter, tried to propose a reconciliation by talking to both parties, his attempts proved unsuccessful. He concluded that he had to "leave matters no better than I found them. It is, indeed, a melancholy affair, and, I am afraid, productive of bad consequences" [Aug. 1779].[167]

The last we hear of Molly Wesley is in an entry in John's Journal on October 12, 1781. He wrote, "I came to London, and was informed that my wife died on Monday. This evening she was buried, though I was not informed of it till a day or two after."[168]

Thus ended a very unhappy marriage relationship.

His glory, to the best of my knowledge, is my only aim, in my thoughts, words, and actions.

George Whitefield

Chapter Two

The Marriage of George Whitefield

"The most extraordinary man of our times,"[1] claimed Lord Bolingbroke. "... he looked as if he was clothed with authority from the Great God,"[2] marvelled Nathan Cole, a carpenter and farmer in Connecticutt. "I ... never had the least suspicion of his integrity, but am decidedly of opinion that he was in all his conduct a perfectly honest man,"[3] remarked Benjamin Franklin. The poet William Cowper penned the following lines about Whitefield, "He loved the world that hated him: the tear That dropp'd upon his bible was sincere, Assail'd by scandal, and the tongue of strife, His only answer was – a blameless life. . ."[4] Soon after his death the Boston Gazette reported, "he ... astonished the world with his eloquence and devotion ... He spoke from the heart, and with a fervency of zeal perhaps unequalled since the days of the Apostles."[5] During the funeral sermon he preached for Whitefield, John Wesley challenged, "Have we read or heard of any person since the Apostles, who testified the gospel of the grace of God through so widely extended a space, through so large a part of the habitable world? Have we read or heard of any person who has called so many thousands, so many myriads, of sinners to repentance?"[6] J.C. Ryle, in regard to the eighteenth century evangelists, gave Whitefield the preeminence, "The first and foremost whom I will name is the well-known George Whitefield. Though not the first in order, if we look at the date of his birth, I place him first in the role of merit, without any hesitation. Of all the spiritual heroes of a hundred years ago, none saw so soon as Whitefield what the times demanded, and none were so forward in the great work of spiritual aggression. I should think I committed an act of injustice if I placed any name before his."[7] And perhaps C. H. Spurgeon, who lived one hundred years after Whitefield, said it best when he declared, "There is no end to the interest which attaches to such a man as George Whitefield ... HE LIVED. Other men seem to be only half-alive; but Whitefield was all life, fire, wing, force. My own model, if I may have such a thing in due subordination to my Lord, is George Whitefield; but with unequal footsteps must I follow in his glorious track."[8]

There are many more testimonies from the pages of history that claim that George Whitefield was indeed an extraordinary and unique individual. Whether one looks at his character, his gifts, his fruitfulness, or the sheer extent of his labors in the ministry, one must admit that he truly was a remarkable man.

In terms of his character, Whitefield stands with few equals. In a day and age where many in the ministry had a "form of godliness," George Whitefield possessed the "power of godliness." The great truths he preached first made a deep and lasting impression on his own heart. His character was marked by his love for Christ, zeal for God's glory, integrity, sincerity, humility, conviction, humor, cheerfulness, and love for people.

He was unequalled, as well, in the extent of his usefulness and fruitfulness. Before Whitefield came on the scene, Christianity was at an all time low in England.[9] Whitefield thundered forth the truths of the gospel clearly and powerfully. Thousands were converted under his preaching. Whitefield's influence extended to all classes of individuals: the rich and powerful, the poor, the learned, the uneducated, slaves, American Indians, children, prisoners, and the nobility. Many men and women who later went into the ministry said it was because of Whitefield's influence.[10] There were twenty ministers in the Boston area alone who said Whitefield was their spiritual father.[11] Many beloved hymns were written by Whitefield's converts, such as "The God of Abraham Praise,"[12] "Come, Thou Fount of Every Blessing,"[13] and "Blest is the Tie That Binds."[14] It was Whitefield who encouraged John and Charles Wesley to take up field preaching[15] and to send missionaries to America. Whitefield's work also contributed financially to the establishment of Princeton and Dartmouth.[16] The revival, in which George Whitefield led the way,[17] swept through England, Scotland, Ireland, Wales, and America. Because the message of the gospel was wedded to social action, not only were individual lives transformed by the power of the gospel, but society was also changed. Whitefield preached the powerful truths of man's sin, justification by faith alone, and the necessity of the new birth. He also exhorted believers to lead pure lives and care for the poor. Whitefield's life and teaching had an enormous influence.

His gifts, especially his preaching, earned him the title "the prince of preachers."[18] His contemporaries greatly admired his rhetorical oratory skill. His dedication to the simple gospel truths coupled with his earnestness, his clarity, and his ability to paint a picture before the eyes of his listeners, convinced people of their need for Christ. The depth and intensity of his pathos touched people's hearts and awakened them out of their apathy. Hume said it was worth going twenty miles just to hear him preach.[19] David Garrick, the celebrated actor, quipped, "I would give a hundred guineas if I could say 'Oh' like Mr. Whitefield."[20] Benjamin Franklin spoke of attending a meeting where Whitefield preached. Franklin was determined not to give any money to Whitefield. By the end of Whitefield's sermon, Franklin said he had emptied his pockets of all his money.[21] Though Whitefield was a "master of pulpit oratory,"[22] he was entirely sincere. He cried for men's souls because he truly loved them.

His labors for the cause of Christ were also immense. During his thirty-four years of public ministry as an itinerant minister he preached about 18,000 sermons of approximately one to two hours each;[23] ministered throughout England, Scotland, Ireland, and Wales; travelled seven times to America, ministering from Boston to Georgia; established an orphan house in Georgia; wrote and published his Journals, numerous sermons, and other works; and carried on a vast correspondence. He, perhaps more than anyone else, is credited with making the First Great Awakening a transcontinental phenomenon. He desired to "spend and be spent"[24] in the work of ministry.

George Whitefield also had a wife. They were married on November 11, 1741,[25] a little over five years after he took his holy orders and began his ministry.[26] Because Whitefield, like John Wesley, was an itinerant minister, his wife encountered many of the hardships common in the lifestyle of an itinerant minister. Such hardships included frequent separations for long periods of time and the discomforts of travelling when she accompanied him. There also were other trials in her life, such as frequent sickness[27], numerous miscarriages, and the loss of a child.[28] Yet despite these circumstances, their marriage proved to be acceptable to both of them. Their marriage, by current standards, could not be classified as a "romantic" or "passionate" relationship. In fact, George Whitefield would have thought romance and passion were foolish desires and had no place in a marriage relationship. However, the letters and journals of Whitefield do not reveal that he was dissatisfied with his wife or his marriage. Early in his marriage, his letters reflect that he thought highly of her and communicates that they were a happy pair.[29] Later, he is aware of her trials and is burdened for her welfare. His correspondence suggests he realized the difficulty of serving God without distraction when one is married. Whitefield's wife did have many trials but seemed to accept this as part of the life of self-sacrifice required of the wife of George Whitefield.

The question arises how Whitefield was able to keep his marriage harmonious while still maintaining his commitment to public ministry. The rest of this chapter will look at four areas that shaped his convictions. They are: first, his biblical and theological convictions regarding the role of a husband and father; second, his biblical and theological convictions regarding his role as a minister of the gospel; third, how these convictions shaped his actual marriage; and fourth, how he, unlike John Wesley, was able to have a united marriage.

The Role of a Husband and Father

An examination of Whitefield's theological and biblical convictions regarding marriage and family reveal that he believed both marriage and family as well as singleness could be honoring to the Lord. In regard to singleness, the advantage and purpose of singleness is to secure undistracted devotion to the Lord.[30] Though singleness does have its advantages, Christ taught us that marriage is an honorable state and not to be disdained. This is evident by His presence at the marriage of Cana.[31] Marriage, like singleness, also had a divine purpose. This purpose was to encourage and help one another spiritually in pursuing salvation. Whitefield believed that God made woman to be a helpmeet for man "not merely for his body ... but chiefly and primarily for his better part the soul."[32] Elsewhere he wrote, marriage is "only in thee, and for thee, to the glory of thy great name, and the salvation of ... our immortal souls."[33] In light of this, an individual must evaluate before God whether marriage or singleness would be best for their soul. A person should choose that state which would best encourage them to grow in respect to their salvation and enable them to serve God without distraction.[34] If two persons believed God wanted them to marry, then by all means they should marry, and "like *Zachariah* and *Elizabeth*, walk in all the ordinances and commandments of the LORD blameless."[35] This was his prayer for his own marriage as well.[36] A married couple should model their relationship after Christ and the church.[37]

Whitefield composed prayers for individuals to pray when seeking God about this important decision. These prayers further reveal his convictions regarding marriage. In "A Prayer for a Man, convinced that it is His Duty to marry, for Direction in the Choice of a Wife," Whitefield asserted that it is God who is to choose the man's helpmeet. As God chose Rebekah for Isaac so God should, first, choose a godly woman for the man and then, second, direct him to her. It was a decisive conviction of Whitefield's that it was God's providence, not the man's passion, which should be his guide. Man marries not for lust, but only in and for the Lord. Thus Whitefield taught a man to pray that God would not allow him to "fall by the hand of a woman."[38] Whitefield knew how easy it was to be blinded by "lust" or "passion" in choosing a wife. Rather than choosing a wife "after thy (God's) own heart," a man could choose a woman who was physically attractive, yet spiritually shallow. Certainly one must agree that many a Christian man or woman intent on serving the Lord has married only to find later that love for God and love for people is sorely lacking in their marriage partner. A bad choice in a marriage partner is lethal to anyone in ministry. Whitefield was cognizant of this temptation for himself as well and prayed that he too would not "fall by the hand of a woman." When he did propose to a woman, he made it clear to her that passion and lust did not move him to propose to her, but rather his desires were for God's sake and by His command. In a letter to the woman's parents, he wrote, "For, I bless GOD, if I know any thing of my own heart, I am free from that foolish passion, which the world calls LOVE. I write, only because I believe it is the will of GOD that I should alter my state."[39] To the woman he wrote, "The passionate expressions which carnal courtiers use, I think ought to be avoided by those that would marry in the LORD. I can only promise, by the help of GOD, to keep my matrimonial vow, and to do what I can towards helping you forward in the great work of your salvation."[40] In our day and age, we might find his proposal formal and unaffectionate. Perhaps the young woman did too. Shortly after, she married... another man!

After a man chooses a woman to be a potential wife, he should seek advice from his friends who are fellow believers.[41] If the man is then certain that God wants him to marry, Jesus is to be called to the wedding.[42]

Whitefield also offers counsel to women. In the

prayer entitled, "A Prayer for a Woman, desiring Direction of GOD, after an Offer of marriage is made to her," Whitefield wrote that she too is only to marry a godly man and only if "this state is best"[43] for her soul. The desire of her heart should be to love her husband only in God, and for God, "to the glory of thy great name, and the salvation of both our immortal souls."[44] In "A Prayer for a Woman lately married to a believing Husband," the wife is to express her desire to serve God without distraction and to "never be so cumbered about the many things of this life, as to neglect the one thing needful."[45] Her prayer should be that God would "keep me from being a snare to my husband" and that God will make her "willing to part with him whensoever thou shalt call him from me."[46] Whitefield lived out these convictions himself in his marriage, and expected his wife to do the same.

Whitefield also held deep convictions regarding the corresponding roles of the husband and wife. In a sermon entitled "Christ the Believer's Husband," Whitefield described the wife's responsibilities. Among them are that wives are to reverence and think highly of their husbands,[47] the wife should "so walk, as to be a Credit to her Husband,"[48] wives are to be subject to their husbands in every thing, i.e. every lawful thing,[49] wives are to be faithful,[50] and they are to love their husband's friends.[51]

The husband's responsibility is described in a sermon entitled, "The Great Duty of Family Religion." The husband's role is to be the head of the house and govern his family.[52] This, said Whitefield elsewhere in a letter, is the harder role. "It is hard to govern; it is much easier to obey,"[53] he wrote. As governor of the family, he was to act in three capacities: "As a Prophet, to instruct; as a Priest, to pray for and with; as a King, to govern, direct, and provide for them."[54] The primary concern of the head of the house was the "Spiritual Prosperity" of those in his house.[55] Failure to fulfill this God-given role was disastrous for not only will their lives be more difficult on earth, but their children will go to hell and fathers will have to stand before the Judgment Seat to give an account to God for their faithlessness to their family.[56] He wrote, "For every House is as it were a little Parish, every Governor a Priest, every Family a Flock: And if any of them perish through the Governor's Neglect, their Blood will God require at their Hands."[57]

Duties to family were so important that even if going to church or other Christian gatherings caused you to neglect your family "you are out of the Way of your Duty"[58] exhorted Whitefield. Family members are to be instructed in the Word of God.[59] He also said that family prayer is so necessary that "if they live without *Family Prayer*, they live without *God in the World*."[60] George Whitefield was certain that "the deep sense of God's free grace in Christ Jesus... will excite you to do your utmost to save others, especially those of your own household."[61]

The father was also to be sure to provide for his family. Whitefield said he was not calling men to leave their families and their "Business of Life." He said when a man neglects his employment "to the Hurt of your Families, whatever Pretence you thereby make for so doing, you are guilty of Sin."[62] In fact, this dishonors Christ more than anything else.[63] A man is even only to help another in his bodily needs, if it does not hurt his family.[64] This raises a pertinent question for us in our day, i.e. what is adequate provision? Leaving one's family in abject poverty is certainly not responsible. But where do we draw the line between the necessities of life and the many modern luxuries and conveniences of life? There is certainly a tension between providing adequately and being content with what one has.

It is important to note here that although Whitefield believed men should not neglect their families, it is still good to spend time helping others outside your family. He believed that if "time is spent upon our own lusts," instead of our families, then this is "exceeding sinful."[65] If time, however, is "spent in the Service of God, and the Good of immortal Souls," then it is not sinful.[66] It seems that between God, family, and ministry outside the home, fathers and husbands are not left with much time to pursue their own "lusts." It is such "innocent diversions" which ruin families, claimed Whitefield.[67] One does wonder how Whitefield would view the average American males "innocent diversions" today ... rounds of golf with his buddies, Monday night football, computer games, Internet surfing, television, etc. It seems likely he would view many men today as leading "exceeding sinful" lives.

As important as marriage and family were to Whitefield,[68] one cannot truly understand his heart without understanding his view of his role as a minister of the gospel.

The Role of a Minister of the Gospel

John Wesley spoke of Whitefield's "unparalleled zeal" and "indefatigable activity"[69] for Christ and His work. Whitefield's own writings reveal the driving force in his life that gave him his zeal. This driving force was his conviction that his life was to glorify God through complete submission to His will in the great work to which God called him – the salvation of "precious and immortal souls."[70] He himself said,

> I hope we shall see the kingdom of God come with power. This is the full desire of my soul. I am determined to seek after and know nothing else. For besides this, all other things are but dung and dross. O my Lord, why should we that are pilgrims, mind earthly things? Why should we that are soldiers, entangle ourselves with the things of this life? Heavenly-mindedness is the very life of a Christian. It is all in all.[71]

Often throughout his letters, he expressed his desire to "spend and be spent"[72] for souls and he claimed to live *only* for the good of souls.[73]

George Whitefield saw that this was especially true for him because he believed that God had called him to this work and therefore he had a duty and an obligation to fulfill. This sense of a call in his life is seen in two ways. First of all, any man called by God to be a gospel minister had certain duties to perform to fulfill his calling. For example, a minister must make sure he himself knows God, he must not preach an "unknown God."[74] Another responsibility was the "Spiritual Welfare of every individual Person under his Charge."[75] A minister's commission is to preach the gospel ... to every creature.[76] Whitefield emphasized, if you are a minister of the gospel, your chief and only concern is to "advance the glory of GOD and the good of his church."[77] Those ministers who say this to Christ, will someday hear Christ say, "make room, angels, and bring up that soul to sit near me on my throne."[78] In a sermon entitled "Walking with God," Whitefield addressed ministers and said they are ambassadors of Christ and stewards of the mysteries of God. Ministers are to be zealous here on earth for in a short time they will enter their rest and "shine as the Stars in the Firmament, in the Kingdom of our heavenly Father, for ever and ever."[79] Whitefield also reminded true ministers that they should expect the "severest persecution."[80]

But secondly, and more importantly to Whitefield, he believed he was uniquely called by God for a purpose. He believed that God had called him to play a unique role in human history. Numerous statements in his journal and letters bear this out. In the opening paragraph of his journal he wrote that even the fact that he was born in a manger in an inn, like the Savior, shows his special call.[81] He also said that even though he led a licentious life in his youth, there were enough of the Spirit's stirrings in his heart to show him that He "loved me with an everlasting love, and separated me even from my mother's womb, for the work to which He afterwards was pleased to call me."[82] From his conversion to Christ, he believed he was called to be "a chosen vessel to bear the name of Jesus Christ through the British nation, and her colonies; to stand before kings and nobles: and all sorts of people, to preach Christ, and him crucified."[83] The day he was admitted into holy orders, he wrote, "I can call heaven and earth to witness, that when the Bishop laid his hand upon me, I gave myself up to be a martyr for him, who hung upon the cross for me."[84] He took his holy orders by the providence of God[85] and by God's grace he was sent out "in the Spirit of the first Apostles."[86] He believed his duty, like that of the Apostle Paul, was to go where the gospel was not yet named[87] and in one letter he claimed that God had impressed upon him that he was called to be the "head of the heathen."[88]

Because God had a purpose for him, Whitefield saw himself as a particular enemy of Satan. At one point when persecution of believers appeared to be imminent, Whitefield claimed that Satan had specifically desired to sift him like wheat.[89] In another incident when he rode into Boston, an avowed enemy of Whitefield's lamented, "I am very sorry, Sir, to see you here." Whitefield immediately responded, "So is the devil."[90] Many concurred with Charles Wesley that Whitefield "shook the gates of hell."[91]

It was this sense of God's call on his life that ordered his entire life and nothing could deter him. Early in his ministry he prayed to God for "a deep humility, a well-guided zeal, a burning love, and a single eye"[92] and it appears he never wavered from what he believed to be his call to save souls. His will, written in his own hand six months before he died, said, "I am more convinced of the undoubted reality and infinite importance of the grand gospel truths, which I have from time to time delivered; and am so far from repenting my delivering them in an itinerant way, that had I strength equal to my inclination, I would preach them from pole to pole; not only because I have found them to be the power of God to the salvation of my own soul, but because I am as much assured that the great Head of the church has called me by his word, providence, and Spirit, to act in this way, as that the sun shines at noon day."[93]

As quoted above, Whitefield believed he was not only called to preach the gospel, but he was called to be an itinerant preacher.[94] Itinerancy, he believed, was prescribed in Scripture by the fact that Christ was an itinerant preacher.[95] He said that it is not wrong to be settled in a particular place, but when "Persons are properly called to, and qualified for, such an Employ" then there is a warrant for it in Scripture.[96] He also was convinced that "whenever there shall be a general Revival of Religion in any Country, *itinerant* Preaching will be more in Vogue."[97] Not only will itinerant preaching be more in vogue, but it is the means God will use to proclaim the gospel. He wrote, "when the power of religion revives, the gospel *must* (emphasis mine) be propagated in the same manner as it was first established, 'itinerant preaching.'"[98]

But not only is itinerant preaching sanctioned in Scripture, but also preaching in places besides the established churches.[99] Initially Whitefield did not intend to violate the Church of England's custom that field preaching was only permissible where there was no established church. However, after the established churches closed their doors to his preaching, he took to the fields. His Scriptural warrant for this was Christ's command to "Go out into the Highways, and Hedges, and compel them to come in, that my House may be filled."[100]

Because of his conviction that he was called by God to preach the gospel as an itinerant minister, Whitefield was willing to endure much hardship. Neither his reputation nor his life were reasons to stop preaching. He said, "I value neither name, nor life itself, when the cause of God calls me to venture both."[101] In regard to his reputation, he said the first thing that he was called upon to give up for Christ was his "fair reputation."[102] Also throughout his ministry he said he experienced "ill-Treatment" from his "Letter-learned Brethren."[103]

His life also was worth risking for the sake of the gospel. Often there was danger from mobs. Whitefield spoke of "stones, dirt, rotten eggs, and pieces of dead cats thrown" at him.[104] He said some wanted "to slash me with a long heavy whip several times."[105] He was often exposed to such violence.[106] But it was all worth it just to save one soul. One man came to throw stones at Whitefield only to abandon his mission. He later approached Whitefield and confessed, "Sir, I came to hear you with an intention to break your head; but God, through your ministry, has given me a broken heart."[107] It was conversions like this, that empowered Whitefield to brave any danger.

The dangers of traveling, whether by horseback or by sea, were also common occurrences in his life. One reads of his "riding hard, almost killed me"[108] and his riding "whole nights ... frequently exposed to great thunders, violent lightnings, and heavy rains."[109] However, none of these were sufficient reasons to deter him from his call of itinerant preaching. He said at one point, "I care not what I suffer, so that some may be brought home to CHRIST."[110] Whitefield would run any risk to win souls to Christ.

George Whitefield kept an enormously busy schedule. His frequent travels on horseback or by sea have already been mentioned. His non-travelling days were spent completely in the work of ministry. He arose early in the morning. If he wasn't preaching, he was meeting with people for counselling or instruction, or he was spending his time in praise and prayer with others. If he had time to himself, it was for correspondence or his own devotions.[111] He even said he worked on sermons while others slept. He frequently said "this sermon I got when most of you who now hear me were fast asleep."[112] As stated earlier, he preached over 18,000 sermons of one to two hours each in 34 years of ministry. He exerted himself greatly when he preached. He usually spoke to 4,000-5,000 people, sometimes up to 30,000,[113] without the use of modern sound systems. He gave of himself entirely when he preached. He said, "I preach till I sweat through and through."[114] One observer commented how at times "he would appear to lose all self-command, and weep exceedingly, and stamp loudly and passionately; and sometimes the emotion of his mind exhausted him and the beholders felt a momentary apprehension even for his life."[115] He gave of himself so entirely that he frequently vomited after preaching, sometimes he even vomited up blood.[116]

His constant travels and preaching wore down his "frail tabernacle"[117] and "feeble carcase"[118] as he called his body. John Wesley, five years before Whitefield died, saw him and said he "seemed to be an old, old man, being fairly worn out in his Master's service, though he has hardly seen fifty years."[119] Often throughout his letters he apologizes for not writing sooner but his poor health and busyness prevented him.[120] As the years passed by he was surprised that he continued to live as long as he did.[121] In spite of his poor health, he continued to preach the gospel. Sore throats were one common ailment. But no matter how sore they were, he said it was more painful to be silent than to preach.[122] He claimed that the best remedy for a "violent cold and sore throat" was "perpetual preaching."[123] Another time he was so sick that he was continually vomiting. When the doctor told him he could only preach once a day (three times on Sunday) until he got better, he said it was to his "great mortification."[124] One time he was so ill that he as well as others thought he was dying,[125] and yet he wrote, "Weak as I was, and have been, I was enabled to travel eleven hundred miles and preach daily."[126] For George Whitefield, if he could no longer preach he would rather die[127] for itinerant preaching was his calling and purpose in life.

It must be interjected here, that Whitefield's suffering for the gospel and the hardships he endured, in no way diminished his joy. Many commented on this. John Wesley said Whitefield "had nothing gloomy in his nature, being singularly cheerful."[128] Once Whitefield saw a print of himself and said if he really looked like such a "sour creature" he should hate himself.[129] One woman spoke of how she came to Christ—"Mr. Whitefield was *so cheerful* that it tempted me to become a Christian."[130] One minister said Whitefield was so cheerful that it made "one in love with a life of religion."[131] Not only was he cheerful, but he was humorous, witty, and "one of the best companions in the world."[132]

His commitment to his pilgrim lifestyle was also evident by his disappointment whenever winter approached and he had to settle in his "winter quarters."[133] He longed to be able to start his spring campaign.[134] Winters always seemed too long. As he entered his winter quarters he despaired of "so little done"[135] for Christ.

His desire was to lead a pilgrim life until he died. He exclaimed, "O that nothing may retard me in my pilgrim life! It is worse than death to me, to be stopt in that."[136] He feared "nestling" and "flagging in the latter stages" of his life.[137] He determined that he would rather "wear out than rust out."[138] He longed to die as an itinerant preacher. After thirty-one years of an itinerant ministry he wrote, "This itch after itinerating, I hope will never be cured till we come to heaven."[139]

In fact, despite being very ill and feeble, he continued to preach the gospel until the day he died.[140] Near the end of his life, he prayed to the Lord claiming he was weary in God's work but not weary of His work.[141] His was an undaunted determination to fulfill his calling to preach the gospel and see souls saved.

George Whitefield not only believed he was called

by God to be a preacher but that he was called by God for a special role in the Great Awakening to be an itinerant minister and if he had "a thousand souls and bodies they should be all itinerants for Jesus Christ."[142] He backed up his convictions both biblically and theologically. Nothing on earth could deter him from his mission to travel and preach the gospel. He was grateful to the Lord that he was able to leave "all that is near and dear ... for the sake of his glorious gospel."[143] It is no wonder that John Wesley spoke of his "unparalleled zeal!"[144]

It was not just zeal for God's glory and conviction that motivated Whitefield. Whitefield claimed it was the love of Christ that constrained him.[145] He believed Christ put the love he had for souls in his heart. He claimed it was love for people's souls that brought him "into the Fields, the Highways, and Hedges to preach Jesus."[146] He also said, "Now, now I live, if poor sinners are flocking for life to the dear LORD JESUS."[147] Whitefield's love for people was frequently mentioned in the many funeral sermons preached after his death. Ministers commented on his "tenderheartedness to the afflicted, and charitableness to the poor."[148] It was noted how Whitefield sought to relieve all who were in any distress, whether bodily or spiritually.[149] John Wesley highlighted this aspect of Whitefield's character. Wesley said,

> Should we not mention that he had a heart susceptible of the most generous and the most tender friendship? I have frequently thought that this, of all others, was the distinguishing part of his character. How few have we known of so kind a temper of

such large and flowing affections. Was it not principally by this that the hearts of others were so strongly drawn and knit to him? Can anything but love beget love? This shone in his very countenance, and continually breathed in all his words, whether in public or private. Was it not this, which, quick as lightning, flew from heart to heart? Which gave life to his sermons, his conversation, his letters? Ye are witnesses.[150]

Nothing has endeared George Whitefield to me more than his love for orphans. He established an Orphan House in Georgia, of which the financial burden weighed heavily upon him. As a result of the burden he carried, he lost years off his life. Whitefield acknowledged his lack of "prudence" in this matter, yet he "found their condition so pitiable" that he had to help any orphans he could.[151] He remarked, "But had I received more, and ventured less, I should have suffered less, and others more."[152] As he reflected on Jesus' last words to Peter, Whitefield said, "... to feed his lambs. It is a work of the utmost importance."[153] Surely his was "a heart bleeding for compassion."[154]

George Whitefield loved people deeply, yet believed that nothing and no one should ever usurp the place of God in our hearts. And for George Whitefield, love for Christ entailed complete obedience to the call on his life to preach the gospel as an itinerant minister. Whitefield said his obligations to fulfill Christ's command to "Feed my lambs, feed my sheep"[155] were very great. He believed "every day lost, that is not spent in field preaching."[156] His sense of responsibility to fulfill his calling was so strong that not even marriage was to hinder this work. About six weeks after he married he wrote just that in a letter. He said, "I trust I was married *in the* LORD; and as I married for him, I trust I shall thereby not be hindered, but rather forwarded in my work. O for that blessed time when we shall neither marry nor be given in marriage, but be as the angels of GOD! My soul longs for that glorious season."[157]

Whitefield's full desire was first to die and be with Christ[158] but if he was to remain on earth he desired to preach the gospel and save souls. From this he never wavered. There was no one on earth that was near and dear to him to keep him from this desire. Even at one point when he and his wife almost died in an accident (she was pregnant as well) he said he "felt rather regret than thankfulness" because he would rather have died.[159] Even after his son was born he wrote, "But why talk I of wife and little one? Let all be absorbed in the thoughts of the love, sufferings, free and full salvation of the infinitely great and glorious Emmanuel."[160]

His son's birth, however, was a joyful event for him. They named him John and Whitefield believed that God had impressed upon him that his son would one day be great in the sight of the Lord and would be "a preacher of the everlasting gospel."[161] His hopes were dashed four months later when his son died. Whitefield's commitment to Christ and His work is probably never more evident than in his response to his having to give up his "Isaac"[162] for God. Within seconds of hearing of his son's death, Whitefield called others to pray with him[163] and he blessed God for giving him a son and then for taking him.[164] He preached the next day even before his son was buried because he remembered "a saying of good Mr. Henry, 'that weeping must not hinder sowing.'"[165] His grief, yet submission to God were evident when he wrote,

> this text on which I had been preaching, namely, "all things work together for good to them that love GOD," made me as willing to go out to my son's funeral, as to hear of his birth. Our parting from him was solemn. We kneeled down, prayed, and shed many tears, but I hope tears of resignation ... All this threw me into very solemn and deep reflection ... but I was comforted from that passage in the book of Kings, where is recorded the death of the Shunamite's child ... the woman's answer likewise to the Prophet when he asked, "Is it well with thee? Is it well with thy husband? Is it well with thy child?" And she answered, "It is well." This gave me no small satisfaction.[166]

He also wrote that he hoped what he had learned through this would make him "more useful in his future labours to the church of GOD."[167] His love for Christ and His work would always come first in his life.[168]

How His Convictions Shaped His Marriage

But George Whitefield did marry and like John Wesley his reasons for marrying were all for the cause of Christ.[169] As mentioned earlier, Whitefield believed the ultimate purpose of marriage was for mutual edification in the great business of our salvation. But George Whitefield had a corollary purpose in mind as well. He desired to marry someone who would be a helpmeet in the great work to which God had called him. Specifically, he wanted a woman who would be willing to manage the Orphan House which he had established in Georgia.[170] He wanted a woman who would be willing to stay and govern affairs there while he continued on in his itinerant ministry. He clearly said that he did not want marriage to hinder his work. In a letter to John Wesley he wrote, "Ere this reaches you, I suppose you will hear of my intention to marry. I am quite as free as a child: If it be GOD's will, I beseech him to prevent it. I would not be hindered in my dear LORD'S business for the world."[171]

Whitefield married that helpmeet on November 11, 1741.[172] Her name was Elizabeth James. She was a thirty-six year old widow[173] who had been a Christian for three years.[174] In a letter to Gilbert Tennent, Whitefield described her as "neither rich in fortune, nor beautiful as to her person, but, I believe, a true child of GOD, and would not, I think, attempt to hinder me in his work for the world."[175] He also said that although he was married, he was "just the same as before marriage"[176] and he hoped that God would never have him say, "I have married a wife, and therefore I cannot come."[177]

It is amazing that their marriage proved to be congenial. First of all, Elizabeth James and Howell Harris, the Welsh revivalist, were in love. But Howell Harris believed he should remain single for the work of the Lord.[178] Therefore, when he heard Whitefield desired to marry, he arranged for Elizabeth to marry Whitefield.[179] Elizabeth consented and it was Harris himself who gave the bride away at the wedding![180] It was ten years, however, before Elizabeth was over her feelings for Harris.[181]

The second reason why it is surprising their marriage was congenial, is that, Whitefield had the same convictions as John Wesley regarding his commitment to Christ being equated with his commitment to public ministry. Because of this commitment, Elizabeth James married a man who desired to live as "those who have wives be as tho' they had none."[182]

There were great hardships in her life as a result of her husband's itinerant lifestyle. There were adjustments to foreign cultures, the inconveniences of travelling when she went with him, and the frequent and long separations when she did not. At one point Whitefield called her his "widow"[183] because he was absent so much.

The third reason why it is surprising that their marriage was cordial was because of numerous personal trials she had to endure in life, e.g. frequent sickness[184] (at one point she was so ill that Whitefield said he found her an invalid),[185] probably four miscarriages,[186] and the death of her son.[187] Whitefield, of course, was not there for her and she bore her suffering alone. As time progressed, she viewed herself as a burden to him and asked for prayer that she would "begin to be a helpmate for him for I have been nothing but a load and burden."[188] Whitefield was burdened for her, but he continued his ministry as before. In spite of all this, the marriage proved to be acceptable to both of them. If Elizabeth Whitefield was unhappy, she accepted this as God's will. She believed that being married to George Whitefield entailed a life of self-sacrifice.

Comparing Wesley and Whitefield's Marriages

The above struggles raise the question why Whitefield's marriage was harmonious and Wesley's was not. The following are four suggested reasons why their marriages were entirely different. Hopefully, this will provide some insight for us in our own day.

The first reason is that although both desired to marry strictly because they thought it would enhance their ministries (i.e. Wesley to break down the prejudice the world had about him and Whitefield to gain a helpmate to work in the Orphan House), Whitefield was extremely clear in communicating his intentions for marriage whereas Wesley was not. One of Wesley's biographers claimed that his wife knew before they were married that he did not want to travel or preach any less just because he was married and she promised she would not slow down his labors. However, even if she did promise this, Charles Wesley recorded she was still shocked to find out his exact reason for marrying her. Whitefield, on the other hand, clearly communicated his desires with the women to whom he proposed. When he proposed to Elizabeth Delamotte, he wrote first to her parents and then to her regarding his intentions. He wrote to her parents, "I find by experience, that a mistress is absolutely necessary for the due management of my increasing family ... It hath been therefore much impressed upon my heart, that I should marry, in order to have a help meet for me in the work whereunto our dear LORD JESUS hath called me."[189] He wrote as well to the woman and asked,

> Do you think, you could undergo the fatigues, that must necessarily attend being joined to one, who is everyday liable to be called out to suffer for the sake of JESUS CHRIST? Can you bear to leave your father and kindred's house, and to trust on him, (who feedeth the young ravens that call upon him) for your own and childrens support, supposing it should please him to bless you with any? Can you undertake to help a husband in the charge of a family, consisting perhaps of a hundred persons? Can you bear the inclemencies of the air both as to cold and heat in a foreign climate? Can you, when you have an husband, be as though you had none, and willingly part with him, even for a long season, when his LORD and master shall call him forth to preach the gospel, and command him to leave you behind?[190]

He also told her that it was not lust or passion that prompted him to propose, but his desires were by the command of God and for His sake. He signed the letter, "Your affectionate brother, friend, and servant in CHRIST."[191] Whitefield was clearly forthright regarding his intentions. He was later informed that she was "in a seeking state only"[192] and thus he did not marry her.

He then proposed to Elizabeth James. The letters of Elizabeth James and the journal of Howell Harris reveal that she also knew what being married to Whitefield would entail. This leads into the second reason why Whitefield's marriage did not have similar struggles to Wesley's marriage.

The second reason is that though both thought it was God's will for them to marry, Wesley's marriage appeared to be in haste. Whitefield, in contrast, waited patiently for the right woman agonizing in prayer over who he was to marry. Wesley appeared to be on the rebound from his broken engagement with Grace Murray, the woman he truly desired to marry. He sought no counsel although he committed to his brother that if he should ever marry he'd consult him first. He also married within days of others finding out he was going to marry. Whitefield, on the other hand, was patient because he knew what he wanted in a wife and was waiting for God to bring her to him. When his proposal to Elizabeth Delamotte disclosed that she was in "a seeking state only"[193] he knew he could not marry her. He continued his crying[194] and secret prayer.[195] His desire was to marry a woman that was "full of faith and the Holy Ghost"[196] and a "gracious woman that is dead to everything but JESUS, and is qualified to govern children, and direct persons of her own sex."[197] He refused to marry if he thought a woman would hinder him in his ministry. Though the needs of the orphan house weighed heavily upon him, he would not marry until the Lord providentially brought a woman of His own choosing.[198] George Whitefield once preached "Some marry in haste, and repent at leisure"[199] and he did not want to be such a person.[200] He continued in his labors, preferring singleness, but believing that it was the Lord's will to give him a helpmate in his ministry.[201]

He temporarily lost sight of his goal to marry and it wasn't until he met Sarah Edwards that his desire for a wife was renewed. He wrote in his Journal that she "seemed to be such a helpmeet for her husband that she caused me to renew those prayers, which, for some months, I have put up to God, that He would be pleased to send me a daughter of Abraham to be my wife ... Choose one to be a helpmeet for me, in carrying on that great work which is committed to my charge."[202]

The third reason why Wesley's marriage differed from Whitefield's has to do with their relationships with other women. John Wesley's relationships with other women made his wife jealous and insecure. This caused great friction in their marriage. With Whitefield, however, there is no indication that this was so. He was courteous in his correspondence with women but not affectionate.[203] When he sensed a woman admired him too greatly he would write to her and exhort her to admire God not him. For example, he wrote, "But here is danger, lest the affections should be too much entangled, and we unwillingly give up the beloved object to our GOD ... I ... hope by this time dear Miss W— can say, my spiritual Father keeps his proper place, and I walk in liberty and the love of GOD."[204] To another woman he wrote, "I only fear that you have my person too much in admiration. If you look to the instrument less, and to GOD more, it will be better. By the grace of God alone, I am what I am. If any good hath been done to you or others, it was not I, but the grace of GOD that was in me. Oh, not unto me, not unto me, but unto GOD's name be all the glory."[205] Ironically, even Wesley in his funeral sermon for Whitefield commented on Whitefield's purity and modesty in his relations with women.[206]

The last reason why their marriages differed is perhaps the most important. Wesley's wife was not a woman who was committed to the ministry the way he was. She would not endure the trials that came her way because of his itinerant ministry. In contrast, Whitefield's wife proved to be a godly woman who was just as committed as Whitefield to the work of ministry.

Both her godly character and her commitment to the cause of Christ were demonstrated even before they were married. Howell Harris described her as a "solid, searching, humble, serious Christian."[207] He also described her as kind and tender.[208] John Wesley, who preached in her home, described her as "a woman of candour and humanity."[209] She, along with one other woman, were the only two women who "conspicuous on account of their godliness and talent ... were permitted to follow the preachers on their preaching tours, to visit the Societies and to write to Howell Harris the results of their observations."[210] Doing this involved danger from violent mobs. She wrote of two such occasions. Once when an angry crowd surrounded her home and another when a mob wanted her death as she came into town.[211] She was a courageous and committed woman to continue to do this.

Elizabeth James was a woman who was unreservedly devoted to the Lord and to ministry. As

Whitefield conversed and corresponded with her, he saw in her the qualities he desired in a wife. She too apparently felt it a great privilege to be his helpmeet in the great work to which God called him. Though she loved Howell Harris, she accepted Whitefield's proposal of marriage. Whitefield knew she loved Harris but because he believed that she was the wife God had chosen for him, he promised "he would not love her the less or be jealous"[212] for, as Harris recorded, his love was "full of tenderness and love and simplicity, taking her as from God."[213]

After they were married, she proved to be that helpmeet that Whitefield longed for. Howell Harris recorded in his journal one year after they had married, "he (Whitefield) again praying and crying if he was to have his choice of all the women in the world, he would choose her."[214] She initially travelled with him and when they did he said they "travelled very pleasantly."[215] She also had a heart for the Orphan House. Whitefield said both he and his wife "have a house that will hold 100 and hearts that will hold 10,000."[216] She did manage the Orphan House for a while until Whitefield decided to make it a seminary.[217] She was very involved in his ministry. For example, she corresponded with people in his ministry, copied his writings on his third visit to America,[218] welcomed visitors into their home when he was travelling,[219] and when they were together she spent much time in prayer with Whitefield for those in his ministry.[220] Harris records in his Journal, one year after their marriage that he had heard how "Whitefield used to spend much time every night with his wife in private prayer."[221] This reveals Whitefield was consistent in his theology regarding family prayer when he was with her. It also reveals that his wife had a heart for prayer and a heart for people.

One sees her devotion to God by her response to many trying circumstances in her life. As mentioned earlier, she demonstrated great courage in the face of danger from violent mobs before their marriage. After their marriage, she manifested the same courage. One time during a voyage it appeared that an enemy ship was going to attack their ship. Whitefield said he was naturally a coward and wanted to hide in the holes of the ship. His wife, on the other hand, bravely set about making cartridges.[222] During the funeral sermon he preached for her after she died, he recalled an incident when he was afraid to preach because of a violent mob. His wife stood behind him, pulled on his gown, and said, "George, play the man for your God." He said this emboldened him to continue preaching.[223]

Whitefield often wrote to others how during difficult circumstances she sensed God's presence. During one sea voyage she had been extremely seasick for ten days. The ship was also in danger, yet Whitefield said she had much of the LORD's presence. He also added that she would be ready shortly for another voyage.[224] Another time, only two and a half months after a miscarriage, she and another woman travelled through the woods to go to the Georgia orphan house.[225] One week later Whitefield wrote, "she is well, and enjoys much of GOD."[226]

Perhaps the best insight into her character is seen when Whitefield says of her that "her Maker is her husband."[227] In understanding the import of these words, Whitefield's sermon entitled, "Christ the Best Husband" sheds light. A person who views Christ as their husband will love the Lord Jesus more than anyone or anything in this world.[228] They will "endeavour to promote his Interest and advance his Name in the World"[229] at all costs. A person who has Christ as their husband knows that "he is the best Husband; there is none comparable to Jesus Christ."[230] Elizabeth Whitefield was such a woman. With respect to her earthly husband, she lived as a "widow." In regard to her heavenly husband, she lived as one who knew that there was no better husband than Jesus Christ. Much credit is given to Elizabeth Whitefield for her depth of loyalty to Christ, her husband, and the ministry. She was an unusual woman!

Concluding Remarks

On August 9, 1768, Elizabeth Whitefield died.[231] One week later, her husband wrote that God filled up the chasm in his life as he lost his "Sarah."[232] Perhaps no other statement best reflects their relationship. Elizabeth was his Sarah and there was a *chasm* in his life when she died. However, George Whitefield's first love was the God who could fill any chasm in his life. Even the most dearly beloved Isaac[233] or Sarah must not and would not compete with his love for God. When they had been together, all was pleasant. They spent much time in prayer and they ministered together. They were "happy in JESUS and happy in one another."[234] Ultimately however, it was Whitefield's ministry that would have his heart. Two months after she died, it was not his deceased wife, but the orphan house which lay upon his "heart night and day."[235]

Two years later, on September 30, 1770, a weak and sick, yet still itinerating George Whitefield, asked God that "if it was consistent with his will, he might that day finish his Master's work."[236] His prayers were answered. He preached his last sermon and retired to his room. Moments later George Whitefield breathed his last and entered into that rest he so often spoke of.[237]

"God requires of us, that we exercise the utmost watchfulness and diligence in his service. Reason teaches, that it is our duty to exercise the utmost care, that we may know the mind and will of God, and our duty in all the branches of it, and to use our utmost diligence in everything to do it; because the service of God is the great business of our lives, it is the work which is the end of our beings; and God is worthy, that we should serve him to the utmost of our power in all things."

Jonathan Edwards, "Christian Cautions"

"the labor of love, is the main business of the Christian life."

Jonathan Edwards, "Charity and Its Fruits"

"Resolved, That I will do whatsoever I think to be most to the glory of God and my own good, profit and pleasure, in the whole of my duration; without any consideration of the time, whether now, or never so many myriads of ages hence. Resolved to do whatever I think to be my duty, and most for the good and advantage of mankind in general. Resolved, so to do, whatever difficulties I meet with, how many soever, and how great soever."

Jonathan Edwards, "Resolutions"

Chapter Three

The Legacy of Jonathan Edwards

A number of leaders in the Christian church believed "the cause of Christ" came before their families. Their influence on their public ministries was extensive, but their families experienced pain and neglect. The prevalence of this makes one wonder if commitment to ministry will necessarily cause one's family to suffer. Fortunately, there are examples of those who somehow were able to have both – a zeal to minister to the world coupled with an equal fervor to serve their families.

One man, who stands out as a beacon in being faithful and a "success" in both areas, is Jonathan Edwards. The legacy he has left to the Christian community is far reaching, yet the legacy he has left to his family is equally extraordinary. Jonathan Edwards and his wife Sarah were married thirty years and had eleven children: three sons and eight daughters.[1] The trajectory of his descendants is truly remarkable. A study of 1400 descendants shows 100 lawyers, 66 doctors, 13 college presidents, 30 judges, 65 professors, 80 public office holders, 3 senators, 3 governors, 1 vice president,[2] 25 officers in the army and navy, and many pastors and missionaries.[3] Jonathan Edwards also poured out his life in the work of the ministry, "spending and being spent" for the salvation of others. Yet he was one man who was able to keep in perspective the tension between commitment to the "the cause of Christ" and commitment to his family. In light of his "success," let's see what we can glean from his biblical and theological convictions regarding the role of a minister of the gospel as well as the role of a husband and father.

Edwards' Marriage and Family

In 1723, Jonathan Edwards wrote these words regarding a young woman named Sarah Pierrepont who had captured his attention:

> They say there is a young lady in [New Haven] who is beloved of that Great Being, who made and rules the world, and that there are certain seasons in which this Great Being, in some way other or invisible, comes to her and fills her mind with exceeding sweet delight, and that she hardly cares for anything, except to meditate on him – that she expects after a while to be received up where he is, to be raised up out of the world and caught up into heaven; being assured that he loves her too well to let her remain at a distance from him always. There she is to dwell with him, and to be ravished with his love and delight forever. Therefore, if you present all the world before her, with the richest of its treasures, she disregards it and cares not for it, and is unmindful of any pain or affliction. She has a strange sweetness in her mind, and singular purity in her affections; is most just and

conscientious in all her conduct; and you could not persuade her to do anything wrong or sinful, if you would give her all the world, lest she should offend this Great Being. She is of a wonderful sweetness, calmness and universal benevolence of mind; especially after this Great God has manifested himself to her mind. She will sometimes go about from place to place, singing sweetly; and seems to be always full of joy and pleasure; and no one knows for what. She loves to be alone, walking in the fields and groves, and seems to have some one invisible always conversing with her.[4]

He later proposed to this young lady by saying, "Patience is commonly esteemed a virtue, but in this case I may almost regard it as a vice."[5] On July 28, 1727, Sarah Pierrepont married Jonathan Edwards[6] beginning what he was later to call their "uncommon union." This union was "founded on high personal esteem, and on mutual affection, which continually grew, and ripened, and mellowed."[7]

Edwards had good reason to esteem his wife. So much is written about her that is positive, that it is difficult not to feel like I border on hagiography. That being said, Sarah Edwards truly was an exceptional woman. She was courteous and kind in her conversation and conduct. It was said of her that she was "remarkable for her kindness to her friends."[8] Those who knew her trusted her because she never spoke negatively about another person. In fact, if she heard someone criticized, she immediately followed it up with something positive about that person.[9] The Edwards household was known for its hospitality due in large measure to the labors and character of Sarah Edwards. Visitors to their home frequently commented on the kindness and encouragement they received.[10] Those who lived with the Edwards for longer periods of time were treated as "one of the family."[11] Besides hospitality, her commitment to others was evident by her ministry in the lives of other women. She met with other women to encourage and mentor them.[12] Sarah Edwards was bright and had had an "enlightened and polished education."[13] Her depth of thought, combined with her godliness and kindness, made her an enjoyable conversationalist.[14] She so sought to please her husband that she did whatever it took to meet his needs. At one point when it seemed he had lost his good opinion of her, she was grieved.[15] She believed her greatest contribution to Christ's Kingdom in her generation was to minister to her husband. It was her ambition to make her husband useful, happy, and comfortable.[16] To that end, Sarah created an orderly and comfortable home.[17] To family members it was a peaceful haven. Visitors, whether friends or strangers, found it to be a place of hospitality and kindness.[18] People loved Sarah Edwards. One minister introduced Jonathan Edwards by blurting out, "They say that your wife is a-going to heaven by a shorter road than yourself."[19] When Edwards pastored a church among American Indians he wrote, "The Indians seem much pleased with my family, especially my wife."[20] But most importantly, Edwards saw that she was a godly woman. As one of Edwards' biographers noted, "so warm and animated were her religious feelings, in every period of life, that they might perhaps have been regarded as enthusiastic, had they not been under the control of true delicacy and sound discretion."[21] She was reverent in her public worship, but her devotion did not stop there. Sarah Edwards sought to bring God into every area of her life.[22] Not only did she understand the great truths of God, but these truths were written on her heart. She loved to talk about doctrine and God's commands. Most of all she loved to talk about God Himself. She spoke of love to Him and His glory.[23] Though at times she experienced bouts of melancholy, overall her joy in her relationship with God was great, and she loved to tell others about the happiness she had in walking with God.[24] Sarah Edwards lived and breathed the truth that a life spent for God and His glory is the most joyful life one can have on earth. Edwards' respect for his wife, especially her religious devotion, can be seen in the fact that he had her record her experience and then he later used this testimony in his writings as his paradigm for what constituted valid and authentic religious experience.[25] Her husband certainly respected and honored her!

Their relationship was characterized by companionship, as well as love and esteem. When Sarah was in Boston caring for an elderly relative, Jonathan wrote a letter to her and addressed it to "My dear companion."[26] Though Edwards was in his study thirteen hours a day, she frequently accompanied him there.[27] They often discussed religion. They prayed together at least once a day. After the rest of the family retired for the night they had a devotion.[28] Edwards was committed to her happiness and her comfort. He said in one of his sermons that husbands were to "study to suit" their wives.[29] Wives were to do the same for their husbands. He questioned his hearers, "Do you make it your study to render each other's lives comfortable?"[30] After staying at their home, George Whitefield said that their relationship renewed his desire to get married. He wrote in his Journal that he was going to renew his prayers to God that "He would be pleased to send me a daughter of Abraham to be my wife."[31] Regarding Jonathan and Sarah he said, "A sweeter couple I have not seen."[32]

When children came along (the first was born one year after they were married),[33] Edwards was committed to them as well. He was an affectionate, tender, and faithful Christian father. His custom was to spend time daily with his family in relaxation.[34] According to Samuel Hopkins, who stayed at the Edwards' household for quite some time and provides eyewitness accounts, Edwards "entered freely into the feelings and concerns of his children and relaxed into cheerful and animated conversations, accompanied frequently with sprightly remarks and sallies of wit and humor."[35] Bills from Edwards' trips to Boston reveal that he bought presents for his family. For example, he bought chocolate, toys, a locket and chain for his wife, and other things.[36] He also often took one of his children on trips with him.[37]

His commitment to his family encompassed a deep concern for their salvation. This was of utmost importance to him. In a letter to his daughter Mary, he wrote, "But yet, my greatest concern is not for your health, or temporal welfare, but for the good of your

soul."[38] He wrote the same to his son Timothy and
said his "chief anxiety" was for their salvation.[39] His
evening discussions with his family often turned
toward this. He was greatly affected by the thought
that they had not yet embraced Christ and at times he
had to leave "in order to conceal his emotions."[40] He
arose at 4:00am before the rest of his family and when
they arose they prayed together and read a chapter of
the Bible. He asked them questions according to their
age, explained passages, and enforced duties. He also
used the Assembly's Shorter Catechism. They were
taught doctrines, learned the catechism by heart and
were questioned on it until they understood it. The
Sabbath was honored. They came together on
Saturday at sunset, sang a psalm and prayed together.
He also brought each child individually into his study
at different times to discuss with them their "soul's
concerns."[41] He exposed his children to godly men and
women. For example, when George Whitefield came
to Northampton, Edwards asked him to speak to his
children.[42]

The Edwards' household was orderly in its
government. Children had to be home by 9:00pm and
they could not stay up long after that when they had
guests. In disciplining his children, he watched over
them so that when their self-will manifested itself, he
could deal with it until they submitted to him.[43]
Hopkins stated he disciplined "with the greatest
calmness and commonly without striking a blow."[44]
He taught them the right things to do and admonished
them of the wrong things.[45] It was his conviction that
it was a great sin not to govern and discipline children,

but he also believed that conflict and anger were not the way family members should treat one another.[46] Edwards gave practical advice here. Husbands and wives, for example, should not get exasperated with the faults of the other because nobody is perfect. Rather, they should seek to cover one another's faults in the spirit of Proverbs 10:12. When misunderstandings do occur, husbands and wives should guard their words, otherwise they will "blow up a spark into a flame."[47] Husbands also were not to be unkind or arrogant in their behavior towards their wives. This too was a great sin against God.[48]

It is true that Sarah attended to all temporal affairs. He "seldom knew when, and by whom his forage for winter was gathered in, or how many milk kine he had, or whence his table was furnished."[49] This was so that he was free to give himself fully to ministry. Yet if she needed advice or assistance he would "attend to it as a matter of utmost importance."[50]

Because of some doctrinal differences, Jonathan Edwards was dismissed from his congregation at Northampton. Before his dismissal he was concerned for his family. He knew that if he persisted in his stance this could ruin not only his career, but also the temporal well-being of his large family. He therefore didn't take lightly his stance, but he sat down and counted the cost. As he did this he realized that "taking up the cross" by holding firm to his convictions might ruin his family temporally, but their eternal well-being was far more important.[51]

In an earlier chapter, we discussed the importance of developing convictions regarding finances and one's family. Here was a man who gave great thought to this. He knew before God it was his responsibility to provide for his family. Yet one thing was of far greater importance. That was the eternal welfare of his family, and that was a much greater priority than their earthly welfare. Poverty and disgrace would be his, yet these were far better to endure than to dishonor God and sacrifice his children's commitment to God. In Edwards' farewell sermon to this church, he called on the people as witnesses to his financial integrity. He did not engineer "worldly schemes" or in any way did he try to advance his "outward estate" or aggrandize himself or his family.[52] He simply sought to provide for his large family. But even that was subordinated if it would affect their eternal well-being.

The result of his commitment to Christ and to his family was twofold. First of all, his children walked with the Lord. For example, Esther's journal and letters show her to be a godly woman who loved the Lord.[53] Jerusha, who died at eighteen years of age, was described by David Brainerd as living a life of self-denial and goodness, more than any other woman he knew.[54] Jonathan Jr. followed in his father's footsteps and became a pastor.[55] Mary was honored by her son, Timothy Dwight, "All that I am and all that I should be, I owe to my mother." This son became President of Yale and led a revival.[56] Lucy was described as "hopefully a pious woman, exceedingly beloved by all her acquaintance."[57] What a blessing to have children that are devoted to Christ!

The second result of his commitment to Christ and his family was that his wife and children greatly loved and respected him. Hopkins wrote, "No person of discernment could be conversant in the family without observing and admiring the great harmony and mutual love and esteem that subsisted between them."[58]

After a visit to Stockbridge to visit her parents, his daughter Esther recorded in her journal,

> Last eve I had some free discourse with My Father on the great things that concern my best interest – I opened my difficulties to him very freely and he as freely advised and directed. The conversation has removed some distressing doubts that discouraged me much in my Christian warfar– He gave me some excellent directions to be observed in secret that tend to keep my soul near to God, as well as others to be observed in a more public way – What a mercy that I have such a Father! Such a Guide![59]

When Esther's husband died and she heard that her father wasn't coming until spring, she wrote to him expressing deep disappointment, "perhaps I lotted too much on the company and conversation of such a near and dear affectionate Father and Guide," and signed her letter "with the greatest respect."[60] He demonstrated his commitment to his family once again by writing back immediately and then he came earlier than the spring.[61]

Sarah too loved and respected him. She had often told her closest friends how difficult it was for her to think of her husband dying. One biographer wrote, "She had long told her intimate friends, that she had, after long struggles and exercises, obtained, by God's grace ... to resign up him, whom she esteemed so great a blessing to her and her family, her nearest partner, to the stroke of death, whenever God should see fit to take him."[62]

If we were to stop here, it would be easy to assume that the reason Jonathan Edwards' family life was harmonious was because he neglected his public ministry. However, Edwards was extremely committed to ministry as well.

The Role of a Minister of the Gospel

Edwards' writings suggest that he concurs with the perspective of those who say that a minister's *entire* life should be devoted to his ministry. For example, he exhorted other ministers to labour "therein night and day."[63] And again he said, "Ministers should follow the example of Christ in his diligence and laboriousness in his work ... So abundant was he in labors, that oftentimes he scarcely allowed himself time to eat or drink ... That three years and a half of his public ministry was so filled with action and labor, that one of his disciples that constantly attended him, and was an eye-witness of his activity, tells us, that if *all that he did should be written, the world, would not contain the books*." He continued, "Ministers should follow the example of Christ, in his readiness not only to labor, but suffer for the salvation of souls, to spend and be spent for them."[64] This echoes the beliefs of Wesley, Whitefield, *et al*.

Furthermore, Edwards tried to live this out in his own life. He did expend himself in his calling. He commonly spent thirteen hours a day in his study.[65] He painstakingly and consistently studied the

Scriptures and other works of divinity,[66] he was fervent in his prayers for the souls in his care,[67] he was diligent to exhort his hearers, during the Great Awakening he counseled those who "thronged" to his study,[68] frequently they had visitors to their home (some of whom would live with them for long periods of time),[69] he carried on an extensive correspondence, he published his writings, and he travelled many places for the work of ministry.[70] After one such ministry trip, Esther recorded in her journal that her father came home ill because he had "tired himself sick."[71]

His diary entry for January 22, 1734 said, "I judge that it is best, when I am in a good frame for divine contemplation, or engaged in reading the Scriptures, or any study of divine subjects, that ordinarily, I will not be interrupted by going to dinner, but will forego my dinner, rather than be broke off."[72] Granted it wasn't his daily habit to do this, but this reveals he was not adverse to skipping dinner with his family to pursue other goals.

Edwards did not take his ministerial responsibilities lightly. To another minister he wrote that "we must be faithful in every part of our ministerial work."[73] Being faithful meant that ministers were to fulfill their calling. Edwards believed God had a design for the church, society, and the world. In *The Nature of True Virtue* we read that each member of society had a special calling according to their talents. Each calling had respective duties that accompanied that calling.[74] To honor and serve God aright, an individual must know and obey God's commands. It is "in the diligent performance of all duties, and in the denial of ungodliness"[75] that one can be sure one is living in God's ways.

Ministers have a special calling and it is the highest office.[76] One duty of the minister was to be an example. Edwards believed ministers "above all other men upon earth, represent his [Christ's] person."[77] He believed that Philippians 3:17 taught that ministers were "to be a pattern for Christians to follow."[78] Ministers are to be like Christ in their self-denial, humility, zeal, love, kindness, in short, their holiness.[79] This was no mere behavioral approach to the Christian life. Edwards always distinguished between mere outward conformity ("the form of godliness") and the inward reality ("the power of godliness"). True holiness of heart and life were the essence of the "power of godliness."[80] One has only to read Edwards' "Resolutions" to see his resolve to lead a holy life whether in private or in public. Edwards' prayer life is an example to us. He loved to pray and "be much on his knees in secret" with Christ.[81] It was his habit to walk in the woods or other quiet places to talk to God.[82] He loved to contemplate heaven[83] and to meditate "on Christ, on the beauty and excellency of his person."[84] Edwards' devotion to the Bible is an example to us. He loved the Word of God and was deeply immersed in it. In describing "the greatest delight" he had in the Scriptures, he marvelled,

> Oftentimes in reading it, every word seemed to touch my heart. I felt a harmony between something in my heart, and those sweet and powerful words. I seemed often to see so much light exhibited by every sentence, and such a refreshing ravishing food

communicated that I could not get along in reading. Used often to dwell long on one sentence, to see the wonders contained in it; and yet almost every sentence seemed to me full of wonders.[85]

But most of all, Edwards is an example in his love for God Himself. Here, in my opinion, he shines brightest. His love for Christ was not only reflected in his labors for Christ, but primarily by his devotion to knowing Christ. Here was a man who devoted his life to cultivating intimacy with his God. He revered and adored God as Lord and Sovereign, but loved and delighted in Him as his most intimate friend.[86] As Edwards taught, the end for which God created the world is the glory of God, thus God's glory is man's most worthy pursuit. God and His glory was Jonathan Edwards' consuming passion and pursuit. Jonathan Edwards truly loved and revered God and found his joy in Him. God was his all in all.

As Christ's representatives, another ministerial duty was to carry on Christ's work. Edwards believed that Christ's work of redemption was his most significant. When Christ rose from the dead, he appointed apostles to teach and baptize. This ministry continues throughout history and ministers are responsible to fulfill the commission Christ gave to His apostles to set up His kingdom.[87] Ministers "especially are the officers of Christ's kingdom"[88] and "the dignified servants of his family,"[89] said Edwards. The minister's task is to care for the souls of those in his care so that they may not be eternally lost:

Christ has committed the precious souls of men to the care of ministers ... Christ knew that notwithstanding all that he had done to procure life for souls, they would need much care to be taken of them, and many means to be used with them, in order to their being indeed preserved from eternal perishing, and actually brought to the possession of life: and therefore he has appointed a certain order of men, whose whole business it might be to take care of immortal souls.[90]

They stand on God's behalf as ambassadors, to speak out in His name.[91] As God's ambassadors, the most important "business and labours of a minister of the gospel" is "to explain and apply the Word of God to his hearers."[92] Ministers are to be fervent and zealous to proclaim God's Word because the preaching of the Word is a means of grace.[93] It is through knowing and obeying God's Word that an individual experiences joy in his relationship with God.[94] The centrality of preaching stayed a conviction throughout his life.[95] It is no wonder he spent thirteen hours a day in his study. He was careful to search the Scriptures with the "utmost diligence and strictness,"[96] meditate on them, and record his thoughts. Edwards felt an even greater responsibility because he believed that God's revelation of His work of redemption was clearer to them who lived in the eighteenth century than in the Old Testament or apostolic days.[97]

Reading through the sermons (including the evangelistic sermons) of the eighteenth century revivalists has been sobering to me. The Word was clearly and consistently taught, and people's lives were deeply changed. It causes me to wonder how such shoddy teaching persists in our day. We are nourished by God's Word (I Timothy 4:6), we are convicted and awakened by His Word (Hebrews 4:12), we grow through the Word (I Peter 2:2), and the Word brings joy (Nehemiah 8:12; Jeremiah 15:16). Yet surprisingly so much preaching and ministry today neglects and undervalues the Word, thereby diminishing the Word's power in people's lives. The men and women who led the revival of the eighteenth century were men and women of the Word, men and women of prayer, and men and women empowered by the Spirit of God. As I've read their sermons and writings, I have been struck by how rich they are in theology and the Bible. These evangelists and preachers boldly declared "heavy-duty" theological concepts like sin, justification by faith, imputed righteousness, and redemption. Rather than being irrelevant and turning people off, revival fires swept throughout England, America, Scotland, and Wales. The Christian leaders of our day would do well to study and apply the "methods" of these great men and women of God. Though dead, they still speak to us. Perhaps our generation may yet see another "season of mercy," as Jonathan Edwards called the First Great Awakening.

Edwards summed up the ministry when he said,

> For this is the very business to which they are called and devoted ... They are his ambassadors ... to awaken and convert sinners, and establish, build up, and comfort saints; it is the business they have been solemnly charged with, before God, angels, and men, and to which they have given up themselves by the most sacred vows ... into whose hands Christ has committed the sacred oracles, holy ordinances, and all his appointed means of grace.[98]

Edwards attached great importance to fulfill his calling to represent Christ both as an example and to carry on his work of redemption. This sobered him to be diligent in his ministry. It was a work of the greatest responsibility but it was also a work of the greatest privilege.

The seriousness with which Edwards viewed his call is seen in his belief that he will have to appear before the Judgment Seat to give an account to God for the souls in his care. In his *Farewell Sermon*, given at Northampton just prior to his dismissal, he told his former congregation that they will appear together "to receive an eternal sentence and retribution from the Judge."[99] Elsewhere he portrayed the scenario of a minister who stands before the Judge to give an account of the souls in his care who are missing. Will he be able to say,

> Lord, thou knowest that I have sincerely and faithfully endeavoured their salvation, I have not been slack nor negligent towards them, I have earnestly watched for their souls, and diligently and unweariedly used all the means with them that thou didst appoint; they perished not through my neglect, but through their own obstinate negligence and wickedness![100]

Those who neglect their calling will incur harsh judgment,[101] but those who are faithful will receive a reward from God. They will be "distinguished in glory,"[102] honored,[103] and given the crown of joy.[104]

All of these things, i.e. the importance of his call, his duty to fulfill his call, and the fact that he would stand before the Judgment Seat to give an account of the souls in his care, weighed heavily on him. It is these biblical and theological convictions that caused him to be wholly devoted to "the work of the Lord."

The ordination sermons which Edwards preached give further insight into how he viewed his role as a minister of the gospel. Harry Stout says in *The Soul of New England* that it is in the ordination sermons that we find his "most systematic statements on the role of a minister."[105] In these sermons one is struck by Edwards' use of vivid biblical imagery. The minister, for example, is a steward, a messenger, a burning and shining light, a "son of oil," a watchman, a soldier, a nurturing mother, a spiritual father, and a proxy bridegroom. An extensive look at each one of these images would make a rich personal study. However, for the purposes of this book, I will only focus on the domestic images because of how these relate to his view of his familial responsibilities.

Ministers, said Edwards, are to be spiritual fathers to those in their care. As fathers, they are to instruct, reprove, warn, and exhort with authority and "with a fatherly tender concern for your eternal good."[106] They are to direct the church's affairs. They are to be an example both in their words and their lifestyle.[107]

The image of minister as a nurturing mother is described in his discursive notes on Luke 1:35 ("Bringing Forth Christ"). In this sermon the virgin Mary represents ministers who work to bring forth Christ in the lives of believers. They care for and feed their spiritual children just as a mother does with her children. He wrote:

The care that a tender mother has of her infant, is a very lively image of the love that a Christian ought to have of grace in the heart. It is a very constant care; the child must be continually looked after; it must be taken care of both day and night. When the mother wakes up in the night she has her child to look after and nourish at her breast, as it sleeps in her bosom, and it must be continually in the mother's bosom, or arms, there to be upheld and cherished; it needs its food and nourishment much oftener than adult persons; it must be fed both day and night; it must in everything be gratified and pleased; the mother must bear the burden of it as she goes to and fro. This is also a lively image of the care that the church, especially the ministers of the gospel, should have of the interest of Christ, committed to their care.[108]

As we see in this quote a minister is responsible to provide the nourishment that his spiritual children require. The minister must cherish those souls in his care. This responsibility is constant. The minister must be available both day and night, just like a nursing mother.

In "The Church's Marriage to her Sons, and to Her God," Edwards looked at a passage in Isaiah which states, "As a young man marries a virgin so shall thy sons marry thee." Edwards understood this to be an image of the relationship between a minister and his congregation, i.e. the minister is married to his church.[109] The minister vows to give his time and strength to the people.[110] Their relationship is to be such that they are to be "the objects of each other's most tender and ardent love."[111] They are to share in each other's joys and sorrows. The minister, as the church's husband, is *continually and earnestly* to promote the well-being of his church. A minister's entire life is to be spent to this end.[112] It must be noted that the minister is not the church's true husband. The true husband is Christ. Rather the minister is a proxy bridegroom until the church is united with her true husband. Until this happens, the minister is to act in the same regard to his church as he would to his wife.[113]

These images once again show the importance which Edwards attached to his role and responsibilities as a minister. It is so important that a minister is to be married to the Lord's work and he is to demonstrate the same commitment as a parent would to his children. His use of domestic imagery is interesting especially in light of our study and how this relates to familial responsibility. If ministry is to be "the object of his most tender and ardent love" how does this relate to having a wife and family? And if he is continually to devote himself to ministry, how does this relate to having a family?

In light of his commitment to be thoroughly devoted to "the work of the Lord," one wonders how he reconciled this with his commitment to his family. What were the theological and biblical underpinnings of his view of marriage and the family as it relates to his role and responsibilities as a minister of the gospel? The remainder of this chapter will seek to answer that question.

Balancing Ministry and Family

One reason why Edwards believed God gave the family, is for our happiness. In his sermons on

Hebrews he brought this out. He called family an "outward enjoyment" and said "we ought to possess them, enjoy and make use of them."[114] It is "very pleasant" to have a family,[115] said Edwards. Family is one of those things that are "very comfortable to us."[116] Although we should be willing to leave our families for heaven "cheerfully and willingly"[117] because "the rest and glory of heaven is so great, that it is worthy that we should desire it above ... husband or wife, or children"[118] yet he wrote elsewhere that one of heaven's attractions is the reunion of our families.[119]

In *The Nature of True Virtue* Edwards once again brought out that family is given by God for our happiness. He said familial kind affections are greatly to our "comfort in the world."[120] This natural affection is implanted by the Creator both to preserve the world but also for our comfort in this world.[121] These "instinctual kind affections" as he called them, lead to esteem (which sees the good in the other) and to benevolence (which desires the well-being of the other).[122] Certainly, as we saw previously, his family experienced the enjoyment and comfort of one another's esteem and benevolence. Edwards derived great pleasure from his relationship with Sarah. Elsewhere Edwards mentioned that he believed "the conjugal relation leads the persons united therein to the most intimate acquaintance and conversation with each other."[123] The husband chose his wife to be close to him above all others.[124] They share each other's joys and sorrows.[125] They do all they can to help one another and seek the good and comfort of the other.[126] "They rejoice in each other."[127] Sarah was Jonathan's nearest and most intimate companion. Edwards also said that God commands "so great and dear a friendship to be maintained."[128] Certainly even Jonathan and Sarah Edwards had situations which called for self-denial on one or the other's part. Edwards acknowledged that duties would be difficult at times, yet he resolved that whatever God called him to do, he would do "willingly and cheerfully as unto the LORD, and not to man."[129] The fruit was a close marriage. This intimacy must have been "very pleasant" to him and his wife. Thus, to Edwards, the family is to be enjoyed. God designed us that way.

This raises some questions we ought to ponder. How many marriages look like this today? How many Christian couples can claim that they have joy in their spouse and their marriage? Perhaps our generation is not living according to the standards set in God's Word? Or perhaps selfishness rather than self-denial is the rule? For those of us who live in America, cultural changes have played a significant part. As Daniel Yankelovich described in *New Rules*, the 1970s shifted America's focus to one of self-fulfillment and the meeting of one's psychological inner needs.[130] This has definitely had an impact on the Christian community. Though my husband and I would both say that our marriage has been a source of great joy, I confess that only within the last few years have I internalized the truth that the foundation of a healthy Christian marriage is not that my psychological needs are met. Rather, the foundation of a healthy and God-honoring marriage is Jesus Christ and obedience to Him. Edwards understood this. Their marriage certainly fulfilled many emotional needs. Edwards clearly taught that married couples should seek to understand each other and meet each other's needs. However, the emphasis is on self-denial for the good and the happiness of the other, not the selfish demands that one's needs be met. Somewhere along the way, we've lost God's perspective and replaced it with our culture's. A godly and healthy sense of responsibility and self-denial have given way to a selfish and barren demanding of rights and self-fulfillment. We must also remember that ultimately the only lasting joy and satisfaction is found in God Himself. St. Augustine's words still echo true, "Thou hast created us for Thyself, and our hearts are restless til they rest in Thee."[131]

Besides the enjoyment and happiness that comes from family, Edwards was also committed to his family because of his conception of the horror of hell. Even children are "by nature children of wrath and are in danger of Eternal Damnation in Hell."[132] He called children "young vipers" and warned, "As innocent as children seem to be to us, yet, if they are out of Christ, they are not so in God's sight, but are young vipers, and infinitely more hateful than vipers, and are in a most miserable condition, as well as grown persons."[133] There was thus an urgency in him to care for his family's eternal welfare.[134]

A third reason that Edwards was committed to his family is because it is the duty of fathers and husbands to do so. On March 16, 1742, Edwards led his congregation in a renewal of their covenant with God. One commitment made to God read: "We also promise, with great watchfulness, to perform relative duties, required by christian rules, in the families we belong to, as we stand related respectively, towards parents and children, husbands and wives, brothers and sisters, masters or mistresses, and servants."[135] This demonstrates that to Edwards, commitment to family was a necessary "duty." Elsewhere in a list of theological questions he asked, "How can you prove family prayer is a duty?"[136] This sense of duty stems back to the Puritan concept of covenant. As one reads Edwards' *Humble Inquiry* one realizes that Edwards accepted the covenant scheme. As an heir of Puritan theology, this theological framework is Edwards' interpretive grid for understanding his role as a husband and father.

The Puritan founders desired to build a godly society. Of the four main institutions: the family, the church, the commonwealth, and the school,[137] the family was the basic social unit.[138] In other words, both church and state were founded on individual family units. The Puritans believed that family harmony was necessary for civil and ecclesiastical harmony. If the family was not strong, this would have a deleterious effect on society and the church.[139] Furthermore, each individual has his place and station in life and is responsible to fulfill this calling. This was mentioned previously with regard to one's vocation. This idea of a calling related to the family as well. Each person was responsible not only in society, but in their families as well, to perform the corresponding duties that accompany their calling.[140] For example, the duties of a husband were to provide his wife with food and clothing, to protect her, to guide her,[141] to instruct and counsel her,[142] to be no closer to any other person than he is to her,[143] and to admonish her to pursue her sanctification. The duties of a wife included submitting to her husband's authority, caring for his needs, and admonishing him to pursue his sanctification (however, only in a spirit of gentleness and submission).[144] Fathers and mothers had their corresponding duties as well. Children were created by God and placed within the family under the parent's care. The parent's duty was to nurture and educate their children so that they would be ready to receive God's grace.[145] It was in the family where religious education took place. Parents were admonished by Edwards to "great painfulness in teaching, warning, and directing their children; bringing them up in the nurture and admonition of the Lord; beginning early, where there is yet opportunity."[146] Parents were also to prepare their children for their vocation in life and in their future calling as parents.[147] He admonished children in their duty to obey their parents. He said that "nothing has a greater tendency to bring a curse on persons in this world, and on all their temporal concerns, than an undutiful, unsubmissive, disorderly behavior in children towards their parents."[148]

The family was considered a microcosm of the church,[149] and thus an instrument of salvation.[150] Edwards wrote,

> Every Christian family ought to be as it were a little church, consecrated to Christ, and wholly influenced and governed by his rules. And family education and order are some of the chief of the means of grace. If these fail, all other means are like to prove ineffectual.

If these are duly maintained, all the means of grace will be like to prosper and be successful.[151]

The fact that the family was a "little church" made family worship important. Morning and evening family worship were characteristic of good family government. The Sabbath being honored was the same. As head of the home, the father and husband was the preacher.[152]

The Puritans believed that if they raised godly children, the church and society would prosper. The foundation of Puritan theology concerning the family is God's covenant promise which he made to Abraham and to his "seed." Puritan children were the seeds of the covenant and Puritan parents were responsible to produce this holy seed.[153] Parents obeyed not only because of God's command but because they feared the curse of the covenant falling upon their children.[154] Thus Edwards was adamant about maintaining family government because this was necessary not only for the childrens' spiritual well-being but for the general well-being of the church and the commonwealth as well.

In Edwards' time, this conception of the commonwealth was fading. Edwards attempted to revive it.[155] This gives clarity why in *A Faithful Narrative* Edwards pointed to the failure of family government as the reason the youth in his time were wanton. Edwards believed if family government were revived, society would change.[156] In one sermon, Edwards mentioned Eli's failure to restrain "his children from wickedness!" The result was God "killed his two sons in one day; brought a violent death upon Eli himself; took the ark from him, and sent it into captivity; cursed his house for ever; and swore that the iniquity of his house should not be purged with sacrifice and offering for ever; that the priesthood should be taken from him, and given to another family; and that there should never be an old man in his family."[157]

In addition, parents would one day stand before God and have to account for the souls of their children and whether they fulfilled their duty to their children.[158] He wrote, "A great proportion of the wickedness of which men are guilty, and that will be brought out at the day of judgment, will be the sin which they shall have committed in the families to which they belong." In Edwards' sermon, "Great Care Necessary, Lest We Live in Some Way of Sin," he said, "When parents lose their government over their children ... the blood of their children will be required at their hands."[159]

Therefore, one can see that to Jonathan Edwards commitment to family was absolutely essential. He saw himself as the preacher of his family, and equally as the preacher of his church. He also saw himself as the husband and parent of his family as well as the spiritual husband and parent of his church. He was married to the work of the Lord and he was married to his wife. He was a father to his family as well as a spiritual father to his congregation. He was a minister of the gospel both in his family and in his calling to vocational ministry.

One further clarification needs to be made. Though

both were the work of the LORD, I believe Edwards would give primacy to the family. For one, though Edwards described the relationship of a minister to his church in the same terms as he described the marriage relationship, he made it clear that there were differences. Marriage is but a shadow, a mere resemblance of the heavenly marriage of Christ and His Church. In the same way, the relationship a minister has with his congregation is a marriage of sorts, it is but a shadow, a mere resemblance of the marriage relationship (and only in some particulars).[160] Edwards made it very clear that the most intimate union on earth after one's union with Christ, was with one's marriage partner.

Second, Edwards himself said, "The nearer the relation, the greater is the obligation to love."[161] Edwards said we owe a duty to all, but especially to our families. Therefore we are not to "neglect and refuse those offices of kindness and mutual helpfulness which become those who are of one family."[162]

He believed he was to be zealous in his call to fulfill both roles. Edwards would agree that one is to "spend and be spent" for the souls in his congregation *and* the souls in his family.[163] Neglecting his ministry to his family for ministry in the public realm was inconceivable to Edwards. He was one day to stand before the Judge to give an account of the souls in his care whether in his congregation or in his family. Edwards desired the eternal joy and honor that comes from God when one is faithful to all that God requires, whether in one's public ministry or one's family. There was no dichotomy because both were the "work of the Lord." Furthermore, his family duties were important to him not only because he was concerned for his children's salvation, but because the welfare of the commonwealth and the church depended on it. This was the Puritan conception of covenant theology of which Edwards was an heir.[164]

For Edwards the essence of his duty both to his family and to his ministry was summed up in the word "love."[165] Love for family "will dispose men to the duties they owe to one another in their several places and relations"[166] and love for people in their ministry "will dispose ministers faithfully and ceaselessly to seek the good of the souls of their people, watching for them as those that must give account."[167] Simply put, "love is the sum ... of all the duties required in his word."[168]

Yet one more Edwardsean and Biblical thought is worthy of reflection. All is subordinated to the greatest good of all. God, who is the most exciting Being in the universe, is the One to whom we look for our ultimate happiness and satisfaction. As Jonathan Edwards expressed, "To go to heaven, fully to enjoy God, is infinitely better than the most pleasant accommodations here. Fathers and mothers, husbands, wives, or children, or the company of earthly friends, are but shadows; but the enjoyment of God is the substance. These are but scattered beams; but God is the sun. These are but streams; but God is the fountain. These are but drops; but God is the ocean. – Therefore it becomes us to spend this life only as a journey towards heaven ... to which we should subordinate all other concerns of life."[169] Herein sums up the man and his legacy to us. Here was a man of purpose, a man wholly committed to the glory of God and the enjoyment of Him forever. Here is a man wholly devoted to the labor of love for the eternal well-being of others, whether his family or the people of God. His legacy is seen in his pursuit of God, in his writings, in his influence in his day, and in the lives of his descendants some of whom walk this earth today.

Concluding Remarks

The familial and marital harmony in the Edwards family lasted their whole lives. When Jonathan Edwards was about to die, he called his daughter Lucy to him and said,

> Dear Lucy, It seems to me to be the will of God, that I must shortly leave you; therefore give my kindest love to my dear wife, and tell her, that the uncommon union, which has so long subsisted between us, has been of such a nature, as I trust is spiritual, and therefore will continue forever: and I hope she will be supported under so great a trial, and submit cheerfully to the will of God. And as to my children, you are now like to be left fatherless; which I hope will be an inducement to you all, to seek a father who will never fail you.[170]

Upon hearing of the death of her husband, Sarah Edwards wrote the following letter to her daughter:

> O my very Dear Child,
> What shall I say. A holy and good God has covered us with a dark cloud. O that we may all kiss

the rod and lay our hands on our mouths. The Lord has done it. He has made me adore his goodness that we had him so long. But my God lives and he has my heart. O what a legacy my husband and your father has left us. We are all given to God and there I am and love to be.[171]

The account in the Boston Gazette of Jonathan Edwards' death read that he was "admired by *all* who knew him."[172] Truly, his was a legacy that is worthy of our admiration.

Therefore, be imitators of God, as beloved children; and walk in love, just as Christ also loved you, and gave Himself up for us, an offering and a sacrifice to God as a fragrant aroma.

Ephesians 5: 1, 2.

Chapter Four

How should we then live

I. Summary

In this book I have sought to present three perspectives regarding marriage/family and ministry. I did so using three eighteenth century individuals all of whom were Christian leaders during a time of great spiritual awakening. John Wesley, George Whitefield, and Jonathan Edwards all believed that the role and responsibility of an individual in ministry was to "spend and be spent" for those in their ministry. They dedicated their lives to the glory of God and the good of others. All three men were extraordinarily fruitful in their labors for Christ. All three men were also married and therefore faced the same tension regarding their zeal for the ministry in light of being married and in Edwards' case, having a family. The way they lived out their convictions affected their marriages. It will be beneficial to summarize what has been said so far.

John Wesley believed that, after God, a man's wife must be the most important person in his life. However, because he saw his commitment to Christ as synonymous with his commitment to the cause of

Methodism, his ministry took precedence over his wife. From his perspective, he could not and would not ever put her wishes before the needs of his ministry, because this would amount to idol worship. He believed that slowing down in ministry was equivalent to being unfaithful to God. The cause of Methodism always came first. This manifested itself in many ways in their relationship. As mentioned before, when they itinerated together and living conditions were difficult, she was not to complain or slow him down. She was also expected to endure frequent and long separations away from her husband. When she went through difficult circumstances in her life, such as the death of her son, she mourned alone. Though it made her insecure and jealous, Wesley maintained close relationships with other women. Even his reason for marrying her had nothing to do with her but was only for the cause of Methodism. She was expected to submit to him and accept that this was his calling from God. Her response to this, however, was one of anger and bitterness. She purposefully attempted to mar his character and make life difficult for him. She would leave him, return to him, and then leave him again. Anyone who tried to defend his character bore the brunt of her vindictive spirit, such as Charles and Sally Wesley. John Wesley could not and would not ever put her before his public ministry because commitment to the Methodist cause was synonymous with his commitment to Christ.

George Whitefield, like John Wesley, also equated his commitment to Christ with his commitment to ministry. He firmly believed that God had specifically called him to the great work of preaching the gospel. Nothing and no one would ever come before God's call on his life. Though he preferred singleness, he believed God desired him to marry someone who would be a helpmate for him in his ministry. He prayed and waited for a woman who would always put the needs of his ministry before her own needs. Unlike Wesley, Whitefield married such a woman. She was equally committed to ministry and was willing to endure much hardship in her life as a result. She rarely was with her husband. She had a number of miscarriages. Her four month old infant son died. If she had any sadness, and I'm sure she did, she grieved alone. Her health deteriorated over the years. Instead of complaining or asking him to slow down, she viewed herself as a burden to her husband. God had called her husband to a unique and influential ministry, and she trusted that God would take care of her. Although they respected one another, their relationship lacked romance. It was a partnership ... a partnership in the great work of seeing people come to Jesus Christ. God and the great work to which Whitefield was called would always take priority in both their lives.

Jonathan Edwards, though deeply committed to his public ministry, also viewed his wife and children as an important ministry. He saw no dichotomy between "the work of the Lord" and his family. Both were the work of the Lord! He believed that faithfulness to Christ entailed fulfilling his "calling" both as a minister of the gospel as well as his "calling" as a husband and father. Jonathan Edwards saw marriage and family as a ministry with corresponding responsibilities and he worked to fulfill these duties. He spent himself for all the souls in his care, whether those in his family or those in his church. He believed he would be judged by God for negligence if he failed to perform his duties. He even believed he was under a greater obligation to his family because of the nearness of the relation. The result was that his wife and children greatly loved and respected him. His influence in his public ministry was great and he left a godly legacy to his family. His descendants still honor him today. I myself know of at least one pastor and one seminary professor who are his direct descendants.[1] His legacy lives on!

Though I have used three eighteenth century individuals, this issue is alive and well in the Christian church today. There are some like John Wesley who put their public ministry first. Their wives and children are to accept this arrangement, but they don't. There are some like George Whitefield who put their public ministry first and their wives do accept their husband's ministry. And then there are those like Jonathan Edwards, who are committed to both their public ministry and their family.

I am sure the reader has no difficulty in understanding which perspective best adheres to my own. I think it comes as no surprise if I suggest that Jonathan Edwards is a solid and Biblical model, worthy to be an example to us. His life demonstrated that it is possible to devote one's life to the ministry without sacrificing one's family.

I think it also comes as no surprise to the reader if

I state that John Wesley's perspective is clearly unacceptable. John Wesley seemed to equate ministry solely in terms of the cause of Methodism. His chief mistake lay in not realizing that marriage and family are also the work of the Lord. His wife's needs were *always* subordinate to the needs of his ministry. He would have been wise to either remain single or marry a woman who had demonstrated a commitment to the same call. There is no Scriptural precedent for marrying solely to enhance one's ministry or in Wesley's case to break down people's prejudices about him. John Armstrong, former pastor and current President of Reformation and Revival Ministries, has this to say concerning five other evangelists (one of whom was Whitefield), who also neglected their wives for the ministry. His words can be applied to Wesley as well. He wrote, "In this they cannot be models for us. True, their times were different, but this cannot excuse faulty biblical understanding and practice. These men failed in their understanding of the covenant of marriage. If we merely blame this on the times in which they lived, then how shall we explain the remarkable marriage of Jonathan and Sarah Edwards who enjoyed a profound love relationship for the entirety of their days together?"[2] We could also mention John Newton (pastor and author of "Amazing Grace") and Charles Wesley, who also had close marital relationships. John Wesley, though a great success in his public ministry, failed in his Biblical understanding of marriage.

George Whitefield's marriage is more complex. His wife accepted his call and there were no children. Yet it is unbiblical and unrealistic to think that if one is married, one's labors would never be hindered. The Scriptures also suggest greater warrant for ministering together, not separately. Peter and the other apostles brought their wives along with them in their travels (I Cor. 9:5) and long separations are not sanctioned by the apostle Paul (I Cor. 7:5). If one does have a family, Philip the evangelist offers an example that one does not always have to be on the move to be committed. Acts 8 records that Philip led the Ethiopian eunuch to Christ and then preached in many other places as well. He then came to Caesarea. Years later (Acts 21), he is still in Caesarea, has a house, and has raised four daughters, all of whom are prophetesses. Philip offers a model of one who "settled." Jonathan Edwards also recognized the difficulties of moving when one has a family.[3]

As one considers how much time to be away from home, the reflections of Billy Graham on his ministry are also worthy of consideration. I quote at length because his words are worth hearing.

> A more implacable problem for my family and me, however, was my constant travel. The only answer was to try to make our times together as normal as possible, and to concentrate on my family as much as possible during the times I was home. Nevertheless, as our children grew, the preaching crusades occupied me, at times almost to the exclusion of family claims.
>
> This is a difficult subject for me to write about, but over the years, the BGEA and the Team became my second family without my realizing it. Ruth says those of us who were off traveling missed the best part of our lives – enjoying the children as they grew.

She is probably right. I was too busy preaching all over the world.

Only Ruth and the children can tell what those extended times of separation meant to them. For myself, as I look back, I now know that I came through those years much the poorer both psychologically and emotionally. I missed so much by not being home to see the children grow and develop. The children must carry scars of those separations too.

Recently, my children have told me that I have probably been too hard on myself. They remember vividly the times of fun we all had when I was at home. Gigi recalls how I used to invent games, especially one called "Spider," and how I played Rook with them, a card game I learned from their grandparents, the Bells. Whenever I was home, I took them to school or met them when the schoolbus dropped them off in the afternoon, just so I could be with them as they went up the mountain toward home.

I now warn young evangelists not to make the mistakes I did. But Ruth reminds me that the situation is different today. There are many more evangelists and far more Christian programs on television and radio, so perhaps the need for constant travel is less necessary. When I started years ago, I was responding to an urgent need in the best way I knew how. And God has been faithful.[4]

In 1978 Billy Graham's wife, Ruth, penned these words as she thought about the sons of fathers who traveled extensively in the ministry,

But
what of the ones
forsaken,
Lord,
even for You?
These sons
now grown
who've never known
fathers who
had undertaken
to leave all
and follow You?
Some sons,
wounded beyond repair,
bitter, confused, lost,
these are the ones
for whom
mothers weep,
bringing to You
in prayer
nights they cannot sleep –
these, Lord,
are what it cost.[5]

After his wife Mary died, David Livingstone contemplated "his shortcomings as a husband and father."[6] He had many regrets and wanted to start over. The sorrows he had put his family through caused him to wonder if he should have just remained celibate.[7]

II. Lessons to be learned and other Biblical thoughts to ponder

What lessons are to be learned from the lives of John Wesley, George Whitefield, and Jonathan Edwards?

What Biblical guidelines can help us develop godly convictions regarding the relationship between marriage/family and public ministry? The following are presented as appropriate guidelines.

1. Being in the ministry is hard work!

Some of the metaphors used for those in the ministry bring this out. People in the ministry are laborers (Matt. 9:37,38), they are hardworking farmers (II Tim. 2:6), and they are to be diligent to approve themselves as *workmen* who do not need to be ashamed, handling accurately the Word of truth (II Tim. 2:15). They are to endure hardship as good soldiers (II Tim. 2:3) and like athletes they must compete (Gr. *agonizo*, from which we get our word 'agony' – II Tim. 2:5). Epaphras wrestled (Gr. *agonizomenoi*) in prayer for those in his care (Col. 4:12). They are to "take pains" (I Tim. 4:15) to fulfill their calling; and they are to be "ready in season and out of season" (II Tim. 4:2). Those who work hard (literally, labor to exhaustion) in teaching and preaching are worthy of double honor (I Tim. 5:17). They are to "spend and be spent" (II Cor. 12:15) in the work of ministry.

No doubt about it – much time and effort is required if one is in the ministry!

2. It is entirely possible that family concerns can be given too much priority.

The greatest commandment is to "love the LORD your God with all your heart, and with all your soul, and with all your mind" (Matt. 22:37). If anything or anyone competes in our affections or loyalty to Christ, then that is idolatry. Jesus said if we love anyone more than Him, we are not worthy of Him (Matt. 10:37). Those who give up mothers, fathers, wives, children, houses, etc. for the sake of the gospel, will be rewarded (Luke 18:29,30). Godly Job was a devoted father, yet he did not neglect those in need. He reminded others that he gave generously to the poor, defended the widow, and that he was like a father to orphans (Job 31:16-23). For those who neglect the outside world and are preoccupied selfishly with their families, there is the rebuke of Haggai, "Is it time for you yourselves to dwell in paneled houses while this house [God's] *lies* desolate?. . Consider your ways!" (Hag. 1:4,5).

Family concerns can be given too much priority.

3. Singleness is a gift and strategic for building up the Kingdom of God.

Jesus tells us that there are those who choose to be eunuchs for the sake of the Kingdom (Matt. 19:12). Paul tells us of certain freedoms one has in being single. "Undistracted devotion to the Lord" is certainly a great advantage of singleness (I Cor. 7:32,35). John Piper makes the point that singles are able to have a "cherished freedom for flexible scheduling and for risk-taking."[8] He goes on to quote from Rhena Taylor, missionary to Kenya, "Being single has meant that I am free to take risks I might not take were I a mother of a family dependent on me. Being single has given me freedom to move around the world without having to pack up a household first. And this freedom has brought to me moments that I would not trade for anything this side of eternity."[9] The prodigious output of men like John Stott is an example of how much one can accomplish when one is "undistracted" by family concerns.

The need for people to devote themselves to singleness is great. Robertson McQuilkin, former missionary and President of Columbia Graduate School of Bible and Missions, says, "Many of the unreached in the world live in conditions that demand sacrifices not suitable for married people, especially married people with children. . .Unless a far larger number of single people make themselves available for that special relationship to the LORD and special service for Him, the difficult frontiers may never be penetrated."[10]

Singleness is a gift and strategic in building up the Kingdom of God.

4. If one does marry, one should choose wisely.

It is far better to remain single than to marry the wrong person. As we saw earlier, John Wesley erred greatly by marrying a woman who did not share his ambition for his ministry. One seventeenth century pastor, Richard Baxter, advised, "'Ought a clergyman to marry?' 'Yes; but *let him think, and think, and think again before he does it*.'"[11] The counsel of J. Oswald Sanders, former Consulting Director of Overseas Missionary Fellowship, in his classic work *Spiritual Leadership*, is valuable in this regard. He writes, "a man must have a wife who fully shares his spiritual aspirations and is willing to make the necessary sacrifices. Many a gifted man has been lost to high office and spiritual effectiveness because of the unsuitability of the wife he has chosen."[12] Many a woman has also forfeited her spiritual aspirations by marrying a man who lacks a heart for God and a heart for people.

Choose wisely.

5. Marriage and family are also God's gifts and strategic in building up the Kingdom of God.

A wife is a blessing, not an anchor to hold one back. Proverbs 18:22 tells us, "He who finds a wife finds a good thing, and obtains favor from the LORD." Ecclesiastes 9:9 says to "Enjoy life with the woman whom you love all the days of your fleeting life... for this is your reward in life." Malachi speaks of companionship as a component of marriage (Mal. 2:14). Edwards, as we saw, spoke much of the enjoyment, comfort, and companionship that comes with marriage.

In the late 1800s, Samuel Zwemer became a missionary to the Arab world. God used him greatly. The hospital founded through his work still cares for people in Saudi Arabia and Bahrain. He described the joy he had in his wife with these words,

> Her love was like an island
> In life's ocean vast and wide
> A peaceful quiet shelter
> From the wind and rain and tide
> T'was bound on the north by hope
> By patience on the west
> By tender counsel on the south
> And on the east by rest.[13]

Certainly marriage is a gift!

Children are also a blessing, not a burden. Psalm 127:3 says "Behold, children are a gift from the LORD; the fruit of the womb is a reward." Leah, after bearing her sixth son, rejoiced because the Lord had given her "a good gift" (Gen. 30:20).

Being married can increase one's effectiveness in ministry and children are strategic in building up the Kingdom of God. Marriage entails partnership in one's life work. Genesis 2:18 reminds us that woman was created to be a "helper suitable" to her husband, as they together "fill the earth, and subdue it" (Gen. 1:28). Certainly the Proverbs 31 woman enhances her husband's ministry, not detracts from it. One nineteenth century pastor, Charles Bridges, said that there are times in the ministry when a man feels overwhelmed. Like Moses, the needs of others will be too heavy to bear alone (Ex. 18:22). It will be his wife, more than any other person, who will "bear the burden" with him. Her encouragement and prayers will be a comfort to him and increase his usefulness.[14]

There is also great fruitfulness that comes with children. One Scripture that imparts a vision for parenting is Psalm 128:3. Children are called olive plants. Someday olive plants become olive trees, and olive trees were a sign of prosperity in the life of ancient Israel. Olive oil, olive wood, and the fruit of an olive tree were precious commodities. Olive oil, for example, was used for eating, illumination, and anointing. Historian Will Durant, in *The Story of Civilization*, says an olive plant "takes sixteen years to come to fruit, forty years to reach perfection."[15]

Though the wait was long, no one doubted that the productivity that came out of future olive plants was worth the time and the effort spent in cultivating those plants. Children are olive plants. It may take years until we see the fruit, and even longer until they mature and reach maximum fruitfulness. Yet the time and effort spent cultivating our own olive plants is well worth it. Not to mention that the inheritance is for many generations to come (Ps. 78:5,6).

Marriage and family are also God's gifts and strategic in building up the Kingdom of God.

6. Husbands have Biblical responsibilities to fulfill.

Men should recognize that if they choose to marry it will change their life and their ministry (I Cor. 7:32-34). Marriage not only will be a "distraction," but certain responsibilities accompany this state (I Cor. 7:32-34). Some of these responsibilities include, but are not limited to: 1) to love his wife as Christ loves the church (Eph. 5:25); 2) to share the Word with her (Eph. 5:26,27); 3) to be faithful to her (I Tim. 3:2); 4) to *live with her* (emphasis mine) in an understanding way (I Peter 3:7); 5) to live with her *in an understanding way* (emphasis mine – I Peter 3:7); 6) to find sexual satisfaction in her alone (Prov. 5:19); 7) to meet her sexual needs (I Cor. 7:3); 8) to provide for her (I Tim. 5:8); and, 9) to be her "covering" (a picture of protection and care – Ruth 3:9).

The purposes of marriage according to Scripture do include partnership in one's life task (in this case ministry), but also encompass other reasons, such as: modelling Christ's relationship to the church (Eph.

5:22-32); companionship (Mal. 2:14); spiritual encouragement (Ecc. 4:9-12); restraint of lust (I Cor. 7:5,9); and, producing godly children (Mal. 2:15). These too are important ministries.

Certainly the most beautiful picture of the marriage relationship are the words, "the two shall become one flesh" (Gen. 2:24; Eph. 5:31). The intimacy of the marriage union includes physical, emotional, and spiritual oneness.

Husbands have Biblical responsibilities to fulfill.

7. Fathers have Biblical responsibilities to fulfill.

Scripture is quite clear what the father's role and responsibility to his family are. The primary responsibility of a father is to teach his children to know and obey God. In fact, Genesis 18:19 says that God chose Abraham for the specific purpose of commanding his household and his children to follow Him. Teaching our children about God involves both formal instruction and teaching as a way of life (Deut. 6:4-9). It involves "bringing them up" (Gr. to nourish them tenderly – Eph. 6:4) in the ways of the Lord. Obviously this requires the father's ongoing presence in his children's lives. Ministry travels away from one's family are necessary at times, but long separations away from one's children would make it difficult to teach "as you go."

Fathers are to discipline their children in wisdom and love (Eph. 6:4; Heb. 12:7-10). As we saw earlier, Jonathan Edwards pointed out Eli's failure in this regard. Eli was condemned by God for his failures both as a priest and a parent. Eli's sons were immoral, and their father did not rebuke them (I Sam. 2:22; I Sam. 3:13). Eli is an example of the truth that a leader of God's Church must "know how to manage his own household." If he does not, "how will he take care of the church of God?" (I Tim. 3:5). Many an individual in Christian leadership has lessened his effectiveness as a leader, because of his neglect to "manage his own household, bringing his children under control with all dignity" (I Tim. 3:4).

Fathers are also to provide for their children (Matt. 7:9-11; I Tim. 5:8). There is no Scriptural warrant or command that for "the cause of Christ" a man can allow his children to go hungry. In fact, if one does not provide for his family, he is worse than an unbeliever (I Tim. 5:8). Fortunately, all three of the men in our study would agree with this.

Fathers are to be an example to their children. Fathers are to "exhort and encourage and implore" their children to walk with God (I Thess. 2:11). John Paton, missionary to New Hebrides, described the encouragement he derived from his father's example, "Tho everything else of religion was by some unthinkable catastrophe to be swept away from memory, my soul would shut itself up in that sanctuary closet [where father prayed], and hearing still the echoes of those cries to God would hurl back all doubt with the victorious appeal, 'He walked with God, why not I?'"[16]

Raising one's children in a missions or a ministerial home has advantages. Children have experiences and meet people that shape their own character. Pastors' homes can be places of exposure to godly men and women. Missionary children have broader experiences by being raised in another culture. Many missionary children I know have the advantage of speaking more than one language (some up to four). Some of our friends have commented that they feel sorry for the rest of us trying to raise children in the United States. The moral problems we face here are not prevalent where they minister. With that said, however, there are conditions that might not be appropriate for a family. Robertson McQuilkin, who I quoted earlier, shares this perspective, "When a missionary discovers that his situation is adversely affecting his children, my conviction is that he, like any parent in any other vocation, should probe the possibility of a radical rearrangement of either location or vocation."[17] His words carry weight because he changed his vocation for his wife. In March of 1990 Dr. McQuilkin resigned his position as President of Columbia Bible College. He wanted to care for his wife, Muriel. She has Alzheimers.

Involving one's wife and children in ministry is important. Bud and Shirley Hinkson have successfully modeled that one can be in the ministry and committed to one's children. Bud had been the Director of Eastern Europe and the former Soviet Union for Campus Crusade for Christ. He and his wife, Shirley, pioneered many ministries throughout that part of the world. Anyone who knew Bud, knew that his labors were immense and his zeal unflagging. He lived and breathed the words of Jim Elliot, "Wherever you are, be all there. Live to the hilt any situation you believe to be the will of God."[18] Bud has many spiritual children, as well as a son and daughter. His son, Jon, wrote a tribute marking the tenth anniversary of his father's going home to be with the Lord. Jon is in the ministry, following in his father's footsteps. He is grateful for his father's influence in his life,

> I thank God for giving me a Dad who believed that ministry was a family affair. It seems like my sister and I were always on our ministry trips. And not simply as spectators, but participants, each having some part tapered to capacity. After Dad would give a talk, when a question was posed he thought I could field he'd say, "I'd like my son to respond to that." Typically, he'd add a coda but over the years he'd append less and less. By then we were divvying up the talks themselves. And so I experienced from youth the blessing of being used of God in kingdom labors. What a gift![19]

Malachi speaks of a time when the hearts of the fathers will be restored to their children. Surely it is incumbent on those in the Christian ministry to show that that time has come.

Fathers have Biblical responsibilities to fulfill.

8. A wife's reticence does not necessarily mean that one should not be in the ministry.

It is true that one's zeal can cause one to run when one should wait. But it is also true that blessings await those who are obedient (John 12:24). Hardship and struggles do not always mean we leave a situation. Romans 5:3-5 encourages us that tribulation leads to perseverance; perseverance leads to proven character;

proven character leads to hope; and "hope does not disappoint."

There is no one right answer for every situation. Each situation is unique and must be evaluated on a case by case basis. In some situations, a wife is reticent because the Lord is using her reservations to give guidance. Martin Luther once declined an invitation to a friend's wedding. The reason he gave was because his wife's "tears and fears" prevented him. She had had a dream that murderers were going to kill him on his way to the wedding. Though he trusted God, he said, "my heart is full of pity for my dear wife Katie, who would be half-dead with worry by the time I got back."[20] Later a friend of Luther's wrote, "It has been discovered that four young noblemen were lying in wait for you. . .Therefore, my friend, kiss your Katie's hand and thank her for, under God's guiding, she has kept you from danger."[21]

In other situations, a wife's reticence is an opportunity to trust God. The following are some suggestions:

− Seek out the counsel of other mature believers, those who know the Word of God and those who know you.

− Realize your wife has a different perspective. Her insight is valid and helpful.

− Understand your wife (I Peter 3:7). Seek to understand her desires, her goals, her gifts, and her limitations.

− Make a concerted effort to ease adjustments and hardships. William Carey's wife may have adjusted to India if circumstances had been a little different.

For example, if he had had adequate funding before he left for India, they would have been able to buy necessities. She might have then adjusted to life in India. Other husbands need to establish proper boundaries with those outside their family. This will help greatly in easing a wife's fears that ministry will consume her husband.

The above are just some of the ways a husband can encourage his wife in the ministry, especially if she is reticent.

9. A note to wives – No matter what your situation, place your hope in God and do what is right in God's eyes (II Cor. 1:10, 12; I Peter 3:5, 6).

Elisabeth Elliot is a model of faith and godliness. Her husband, Jim, was one of five missionaries who sought to bring the gospel to the Auca Indians. In their attempt, they were martyred. In her book, *Let Me Be a Woman*, she wrote, "We are called to be women. The fact that I am a woman does not make me a different kind of Christian, but the fact that I am a Christian does make me a different kind of woman. For I have accepted God's idea of me, and my whole life is an offering to Him of all that I am and all that He wants me to be." The following are some suggested ways we can offer our lives in trust and obedience to God.

– Recognize that it is only in Jesus Christ that your deepest needs are met. It is inherently impossible for your husband to do this because he is a finite and fallen being. Only God, who is an infinite being, is capable of meeting one's deepest needs. Some husbands meet many needs, but no husband can meet all one's needs.

Lila Trotman had been the wife of Dawson Trotman, founder of the Navigators. Her husband died trying to rescue someone who was drowning. Lila Trotman once gave this counsel, "always remember that God is your only circumstance."[23] Her words teach us that whatever circumstance we find ourselves in, God is there too.

– Seek to understand your husband: his needs, his desires, his weaknesses, his moods, his sources of discouragement, in short, everything. The marital counsel of Jonathan Edwards is an encouragement to "study to suit" one's husband. Sarah Edwards applied this in her marriage. It is no wonder that Thomas Woolsley, descendant of the Edwards and President of Yale in the late 1800s, remarked, "Sarah had been the resting place of Jonathan's soul."[24]

My husband enjoys a well-ordered home. It is a priority to me to see that he gets it. He also likes the car cleaned out. That has been a bit more difficult, but I am working on it!

Martin Luther struggled throughout his life with depression. When those times hit, his wife either read Scripture to him or invited a friend over who could make him happy.[25] This wise wife understood her husband. He loved and valued her, calling her his "greatest blessing. . .a very empress."[26]

– Find out the ministry God has for you. God's Word instructs us that our main ministry is to our husband and children (Titus 2:4). God has also given each one of us gifts with which to serve the Body (I Cor. 12:7). One's season of life also helps to determine how much one can give outside the home.

– Cultivate a thankful heart. It is a great assurance to

know that in any and every situation, God has revealed His will to us. God's will is, "in everything give thanks, for this is God's will for you in Christ Jesus (I Thess. 5:18). For wives, "in everything" includes our husbands.

I once heard Barbara Rainey share her thoughts on marriage. Barbara is the wife of Dennis Rainey, who heads up "Family Life Ministries." Barbara shared how she used to complain about her husband's weaknesses and sins. She became convicted of this, stopped complaining, and started to pray that God would change her husband. She soon realized that that kept her focus on her husband's negative qualities. She decided to make a list of what she appreciated about her husband. She then spent her prayer time thanking the Lord for those positive qualities she saw in her husband. Just this one principle alone will change your entire outlook on your husband.

Wives, place your hope in God and do what is right in God's eyes.

10. An individual in the ministry must be circumspect in how he treats women other than his wife.

I mentioned earlier, that Molly Wesley's greatest struggle was her husband's apparent affection for women to which he sought to minister. I personally cannot think of one woman I know who would not have had the same struggle. Understanding one's wife (I Peter 3:7) involves understanding how she feels in this area.

I Timothy 3:2 says a man in Biblical leadership must be "the husband of one wife." There is some debate regarding what exactly this means, but one thing is clear. The man of God must have eyes for one woman only and that woman is his wife. He must be blameless in his conduct with other women.

I Thessalonians 5:22 sets further boundaries. We are to avoid *any* appearance of evil. One prominent pastor, Chuck Swindoll, commented that certain women would describe him as cold and aloof. I also recall one radio program where he disparaged silly games that married people play, like flirting with individuals to whom they are not married.

The first responsibility listed in I Timothy 3 regarding the qualification of a leader in God's church is that he must be "above reproach." Certainly, he must seek to be "above reproach" in the eyes of his wife, as well as others.

An individual in the ministry must be circumspect in how he treats women other than his wife.

11. There is always time to do what God requires.

John R. Mott was one of the leaders of the Student Volunteer Movement. This was a massive missionary outreach at the turn of the nineteenth/twentieth century. Mott wrote down lessons he had learned over the fifty years that he sought to establish ministries/movements. One lesson he learned was,

> In any work abounding in pressing needs and great opportunities, we must make a study of priorities. We must plan the use of our time. No man can do:
> A - all the good that needs to be done;
> B - all that others want him to do;
> C - all that he himself wants to do.
> Therefore, he must acquire the habit of putting first things first.[27]

His counsel reminds us that we must live by priorities. Urgent needs will swallow up the important, unless we plan otherwise. Good things must not be allowed to usurp the place of excellent things (Phil. 1:9-11).

I would like to add, that although we do not have the time to do everything, there is always enough time to do what God requires. J. Oswald Sanders reminds us it is possible to balance family and ministry. In commenting on I Tim. 3:4,5, he states, "The clear implicaton is that, while caring for the interests of the church or other spiritual activity, the leader will not neglect the family, which is his personal and primary responsibility. In the economy of God, the discharge of one God-given duty or responsibility will never involve the neglect of another."[28]

There is always enough time to do what God requires.

12. Motives count because God sees the heart (I Sam. 16:7).

Ambition can be godly (II Cor. 5:9; Rom. 15:20). Selfish ambition is ungodly. Selfish ambition can be just as prevalent in the ministry as on Wall Street. James 4:3 speaks of the root of selfish ambition. It is wanting what we want so that we may "spend it on our own pleasures" (i.e. self-gratification). If one's drive in ministry stems from the need for approval, the need to be recognized, or a desire to be loved and admired, then one is treading on dangerous ground. If one is seeking to build his own kingdom, then selfish ambition is the culprit. It was the habit of Jonathan

Edwards to examine himself daily to make certain he was living for God, rather than for any earthly motive.[29] When he was asked to leave his church in Northampton, he could say with all integrity that he labored night and day for God's glory and the good of others, not for his own temporal welfare.[30]

In contrast to selfish ambition there are three godly motives in Scripture: fear of God, love for Christ, and the desire for rewards (II Cor. 5:10-14).

Motives count because God sees the heart.

13. The bottom line is obedience to God's commands.

To say, "but look how much good has come in other people's lives from choosing ministry over one's family," is not valid. It is true that tremendous good has come from the lives of men like William Carey, David Livingstone, John Wesley, et al. For this, we must hold men like them in high regard (Phil. 2:29). But we must remember, we only know what happened. We do not know what would have happened if another course was followed.[31] We saw earlier, that if Charles Wesley had not slowed down his labors for his family, the church would not have the rich heritage of his hymns.

This is also true for another married couple. They dreamed of doing missions work and went to Mexico. It was soon found out that the woman had a heart condition. They both gave up their dream of serving the Lord in Mexico and instead decided to serve Him in the United States where she could get the medical care she needed. It turned out to be a fruitful decision because by coming home, the wife Kay, poured herself into another ministry. Her ministry has helped many discover the power of God's Word in their lives. The woman is Kay Arthur, founder of Precepts ministries.

The bottom line is obedience.

CONCLUDING THOUGHTS

Leaving a legacy in Marriage and Ministry

"Let us in our married relationships show how Christ binds together two persons in holy love ... let us so live in this relationship that people of the world looking at us shall say, 'Would to God we could live like that; would to God we were as happy as they are ...'"

D. Martin Lloyd-Jones, *The Life of Joy*

May our lives glorify God as we seek to fulfill *all* the ministry He has given to us. May the blessing be upon "our children's children!" May His love extend each legacy to the thousandth generation!

Endnotes

Introduction

1. Ruth Tucker, *From Jerusalem to Irian Jaya: A Biographical History of Christian Missions* (Grand Rapids, Mich.: Zondervan, 1983), 264-7. I am indebted to this work for the above summary of C.T. Studd.

2. Ibid., 266.

3. Ibid., 116.

4. Timothy George, *The Life and Mission of William Carey* (Birmingham, Alabama: New Hope, 1991), 88.

5. Mark Galli, "The Man Who Wouldn't Give Up," *Christian History* 36 (Vol. XI, No. 4): 13.

6. Ibid.

7. Ibid., 13,14.

8. Ibid.

9. Ruth Tucker, *From Jerusalem to Irian Jaya*, 117.

10. Alvyn Austin, "Discovering Livingstone: The Man, The Missionary, The Explorer, The Legend," *Christian History* 56 (Vol. XVI, No. 4): 14.

11. Elizabeth Isichei, "The Man with Three Wives," *Christian History* 56 (Vol. XVI, No. 4): 29.

12. Ibid.

13. Alvyn Austin, "Discovering Livingstone," 14.

14. Elizabeth Isichei, "The Man With Three Wives," 29.

15. Ibid.

16. Ruth Tucker, *From Jerusalem to Irian Jaya*, 150.

17. Alvyn Austin, "Discovering Livingstone," 18.

18. Ruth Tucker, *From Jerusalem to Irian Jaya*, 151.

19. Elizabeth Isichei, "The Man with Three Wives," 29.

20. Elizabeth Isichei, "David Livingstone, Missionary Explorer," *Christian History* 56 (Vol. XVI, No. 4): 26.

21. Elizabeth Isichei, "The Man With Three Wives," 30.

22. Ibid.

23. Alvyn Austin, "Discovering Livingstone," 18.

24. Elizabeth Isichei, "The Man With Three Wives," 30.

25. Ruth Tucker, "Did You Know?" *Christian History* 56 (Vol. XVI, No. 4): 2.

26. Evangeline Anderson-Rajkumar, "Ministry in the Killing Fields," *Christian History* 36 (Vol. XI, No. 4): 35.

27. R.E. Hedland, "Did You Know?" *Christian History* 36 (Vol. XI, No. 4): 2.

28. These questions presuppose the complementary view of marriage.

29. A Skevington Wood, "John and Charles Wesley and Methodism," in *Great Leaders of the Christian Church*, ed. John D. Woodbridge (Chicago: Moody Press, 1988), 287.

30. Ibid., 290.

31. John Wesley, *An Extract of the Rev. Mr. John Wesley's Journal*, in *The Works of John Wesley*, vol. 1 (Peabody, Massachusetts: Hendrickson Publishers, 1991; reprint, London: Wesleyan Methodist Book Room, 1872), 75-76.

32. Ibid., 103.

33. John D. Woodbridge, a lecture delivered on John Wesley at Trinity Evangelical Divinity School on March 12, 1991.

34. A. Skevington Wood, "John and Charles Wesley and Methodism," 293-294.

35. John D. Woodbridge, a lecture delivered on John Wesley at Trinity Evangelical Divinity School on March 12, 1991.

36. A. Skevington Wood, "John and Charles Wesley and Methodism," 287.

37. George Whitefield, *George Whitefield's Journals* (Edinburgh: The Banner of Truth Trust, 1989; reprint from the 1960 ed.), 21.

38. Ibid., 38.

39. Ibid., 46.

40. Ibid., 47.

41. Ibid.

42. Ibid.

43. Ibid., 70.

44. Arnold A. Dallimore, "George Whitefield: English Evangelist," in *Great Leaders of the Christian Church*, 295.

45. Susan O'Brien, "A Transatlantic Community of Saints: The Great Awakening and the First Evangelical Network, 1735-1755," *American Historical Review* 91 (1986).

46. Backcover of *George Whitefield's Journals*.

47. Arnold A. Dallimore, "George Whitefield: English Evangelist," 295.

48. Ibid.

49. Sereno E. Dwight, "Memoirs of Jonathan Edwards," in *The Works of Jonathan Edwards*, ed. Edward Hickman (Edinburgh: The Banner of Truth Trust, 1990; reprint, 1974 ed.), 1:xi.

50. Ibid.

51. Ibid., xiii.

52. Ibid., xiv.

53. Ibid., xliii.

Endnotes

54. Jonathan Edwards, "A Faithful Narrative of the Surprising Work of God," in *The Works of Jonathan Edwards*, 350.
55. Dwight, "Memoirs," xlix.
56. Ibid., cxvi-cxvii.
57. Ibid., cxxviii.
58. Ibid., clxiii.
59. Ibid., clxxiii.
60. Ibid., clxxviii.
61. Jonathan Edwards, "Resolutions," in *The Works of Jonathan Edwards*, xx.
62. Ibid.

Chapter 1 - The Marriage of John Wesley

1. There is a discrepancy between two magazines as to the date. The *Gentleman's Magazine* states: "Feb. 18th-Rev. Mr. John Wesley, Methodist preacher, to a merchant's widow in Threadneedle Street, with a jointure of £300 per annum." The *London Magazine* states: "Feb. 19th-Rev. Mr. John Wesley, to Mrs. Vazel, of Threadneedle Street, a widow lady of large fortune." Rev. L. Tyerman, *The Life and Times of the Rev. John Wesley*, vol. 2 (New York: Harper and Brothers, Publishers, 1872), 101.
2. Whether the children were young or grown is hard to say. There is insufficient evidence in primary sources and discrepancies in secondary sources. I think there is greater evidence to say that some were young and some were grown.
3. In a letter to his friend Ebenezer Blackwell, Wesley asks him to assist with his wife's financial affairs. Samuel Lloyd had drawn up a financial arrangement securing Molly's fortune to herself and her children. John Wesley, *The Letters of John Wesley*, ed. John Telford (London: The Epworth Press, 1931), 3:66-67.
4. Charles Wesley, *The Journal of the Rev. Charles Wesley with Selections from His Correspondence and Poetry*, ed. Thomas Jackson, with an introduction and occasional notes by Thomas Jackson (London: John Mason, 1849), 78.
5. John Wesley, *The Journal of the Rev. John Wesley*, ed. Nehemiah Curnock (London: The Epworth Press, 1912; reprint), 3:512-3 (page numbers are to reprint edition).
6. *Wesley's Works*, vol. v, 205, quoted in Tyerman, *Life and Times*, 2:108.
7. John Wesley, *Letters*, 4:143-4.
8. *MS Letter* as quoted in Tyerman, *Life and Times*, 2:113.
9. John Wesley, *Journal of John Wesley*, 5:399-400.
10. Luke Tyerman, *The Life and Times of the Rev. John Wesley*, 2:106.
11. Hampson as quoted in ibid., 2:102.
12. Mabel Richmond Brailsford, *A Tale of Two Brothers: John and Charles Wesley* (Soho Square, London: Rupert hart-Davis, 1954), 230.
13. John Telford, *The Life of John Wesley* (London: Wesleyan Methodist

Book Room, Paternoster Row, 1899), 252.

14. Henry Moore, *The Life of the Rev. John Wesley* (New York: N. Bangs and J. Emory, 1826), 2:105.

15. V.H.H. Green, *John Wesley* (London and Edinburgh: Thomas Nelson, 1964), 104.

16. Stanley Ayling, *John Wesley* (Collins: St James Place, London, 1979), 230.

17. Hampson as quoted in Tyerman, *The Life and Times of the Rev. John Wesley*, 2:102.

18. Whitehead's *Life of Wesley* as quoted in Tyerman, 2:103.

19. John Wesley, "On Family Religion," In *The Works of John Wesley*, vol. 7 (Peabody, Massachusetts: Hendrickson Publishers, 1991; reprint, London: Wesleyan Methodist Book Room, 1872), 78-79 (page references are to reprint edition). This sermon was first published in the *Arminian Magazine* on May 26, 1783. It is not known whether this sermon was composed or preached at an earlier date. Albert C. Outler, ed., *The Works of John Wesley* (Nashville: Abingdon Press, 1986), 3:643.

20. John Wesley, "Duties of Husbands and Wives," in *The Works of the Rev. John Wesley*, vol. 9 (London: n.p., 1811), 55-91.

21. John Wesley, *Wesley's Notes on the Bible* (Grand Rapids, Michigan: Francis Asbury Press, 1987), 538.

22. Wesley, "On Family Religion," 7:78-79.

23. John Wesley, "On Friendship with the World," In *The Works of John Wesley*, vol. 6 (Peabody, Massachusetts: Hendrickson Publishers, 1991; reprint, London: Wesleyan Methodist Book Room, 1872), 462. This sermon was published in the *Arminian Magazine* on May 1, 1786. It is not known whether this sermon was composed or preached at an earlier date. Outler, *The Works of John Wesley*, 3:644.

24. John Wesley, "On Family Religion," 7:81. Emphasis added.

25. Ibid., 7:82.

26. See footnote 2.

27. Augustin Leger, *John Wesley's Last Love* (London:J.M. Dent & Sons Ltd., 1910), 69. In this book is John Wesley's journal regarding his relationship with Grace Murray. All my quotes are taken directly from Wesley's manuscript.

28. Telford, *Letters*, 4:322.

29. Brailsford, *A Tale of Two Brothers*, 230.

30. John Wesley, "Spiritual Idolatry" in *The Works of John Wesley* vol. 6 (Peabody, Massachusetts: Hendrickson Publishers, 1991; reprint), 441.

31. John Wesley, *Letters*, 4:101. Emphasis added.

32. John Wesley, *Letters*, 3:100.

33. John Wesley, "Thoughts on a Single Life" (London: G. Paramore, 1793), 1-11.

34. John Wesley, *Journal*, 3:512.

35. John Wesley, *Journal*, 5:101.

36. John Wesley, *Journal*, 3:517.

37. The letter was to William Orpe. They ended up with a happy marriage. John Wesley, *Letters*, 5:62-63.

38. John Wesley, in *The Works of John Wesley*, 2:223.

39. John Wesley, *Journal*, 5:282.

40. JW's MSS in Leger, *John Wesley's Last Love*, 68.

41. John Wesley, *Journal*, 3:512.

42. *The Journal of Charles Wesley* as quoted in John Wesley, *Journal*, 3:515. Wesleyan scholar, Robert G. Tuttle, told me that the prejudice is probably related to a standard in the Anglican Church (a private conversation in 1992, specific date unrecalled.)

43. Ibid. The context indicates that she was surprised to hear this.

44. John Wesley, *Letters*, 3:15-18.

45. Leger, *John Wesley's Last Love*, pp. 38, 52, 58.

46. She writes at 77 years of age, recalling her ministry 50 years earlier, "I have known the time, when I have been joining in the praises of my LORD with his people at four o'clock in the morning; and I continued all day from one place of devotion to another, without faintness." William Bennet, *Memoirs of Mrs. Grace Bennet* (Macclesfield: Bayley, 1803), 19,53.

47. JW's MSS in Leger, *John Wesley's Last Love*, 70.

48. Ibid., 72.

49. Ibid., 71.

50. Ibid., 72.

51. Ibid., 73.

52. Ibid., 70-72.

53. Ibid., 73.

54. Extracts from the British Museum MS as quoted in John Wesley, *Journal*, 3:435-9.

55. JW's MSS in Leger, *John Wesley's Last Love*, 65-66.

56. Ibid., 64.

57. Ibid., 64. She was a "servant" and "low-born." This was "shocking" to Charles.

58. Ibid., 66, 77.

59. Ibid., 5, 77-78.

60. Ibid., 8, 9, 88-89. See also John Wesley, *Letters*, 3:19.

61. Ibid., 87.

62. Ibid., 88.

63. Ibid., 70.

64. Ibid., 61.

65. Ibid., 62.

66. John Bennet was also an itinerant Methodist preacher who later became a Calvinist. Grace bore five sons to John Bennet, one of whom became a Congregational minister. After ten years of marriage, John Bennet died. Grace immediately rejoined the Methodists. She never remarried. Twenty-six years later she wrote of her husband that "without the enjoyment of

his love everything is poor and empty." In the same letter she says of Wesley, "I love and honor him as a father." In 1788, she and Wesley met for the last time. In 1796, at 85 years old, she wrote, "suffer not to live a day longer than is for thy glory, to live is Christ But to die is gain..." Three years later in 1799, Grace Bennet died. The church register said, "She was a real pious saint of Christ for 63 years." Looking at her life, I have to agree that this was a fit description of her. Perhaps she would have made Wesley an excellent wife, but it was not meant to be.

67. Ibid., 98ff.
68. Ibid., 83.
69. Charles Wesley, *Journal*, 78.
70. Ibid., 44.
71. Ibid.
72. Ibid., 78.
73. JW's MSS in Leger, *John Wesley's Last Love*, 73.
74. John Wesley, *Wesley's Notes on the Bible*, 311.
75. Henry Moore, *The Life of the Rev. John Wesley*, 103.
76. *Works*, vol. xii, 114 as quoted in John Wesley, *Journal*, 4:87.
77. Henry Moore, *The Life of the Rev. John Wesley*, vol. 2 (London: Paternoster Row, 1825), 173.
78. John Wesley, *Journal*, 4:11-12.
79. Letter, July 20, 1755.
80. John Wesley, *Letters*, 3:87.
81. John Wesley, *Journal*, 4:21.
82. Frank Baker, *The Works of John Wesley*, vol. 26, *Letters 1740-1755* (Oxford: Clarendon Press, 1982), 497.
83. Ibid., 495 (See Footnote 8).
84. John Wesley, *Journal*, 4:92.
85. John Wesley, *Works*, vol. 26, *Letters 1740-1755*, 581.
86. John Wesley, *Journal*, 4:84 (See Wesley's entry and footnote 2).
87. John Wesley, *Letters*, 4:101.
88. Ibid. Earlier Wesley wrote to Molly, "Indeed, He mingles afflictions with your cup. But may not these be blessings also? May they not be admirable means to break the impetuosity and soften the harshness of your spirit?" [April 24, 1761]. Wesley, *Letters*, 4:152-3.
89. John Wesley, *Letters*, 3:66.
90. Wesley writes to Ebenezer Blackwell concerning this on Sept. 12, 1755. He writes, "Charles Perronet being out of town last Saturday, my packet directed to him fell into other hands (Wesley's wife's). This has raised a violent storm. For it contained a few lines I writ [sic] to Mrs. LeFevre, in answer to a letter she sent me the week before, concerning Mr. Furly. So now 'all the intrigue is discovered, and the reason why I direct my letters to Mr. Perronet'. 'Tis pity! I should be glad if I had to do with reasonable people. But this likewise is for good." Wesley, *Works*, 26:586-7.
91. Ibid., 26:461 (Footnote 19 quotes his MS Journal).

92. One biographer, Maldwyn Edward, claimed it was customary to address women in such language. Maldwyn Edward, *My Dear Sister: The Story of John Wesley and the Women in His Life* (Manchester: Penwork Ltd., n.d.), 112. My research into eighteenth century social history did not confirm nor deny this. However, two points need to be considered. First, a comparison with George Whitefield reveals that Wesley's free and affectionate communication was not necessary. Whitefield corresponded with many women yet his language demonstrated a deep commitment without being so forward and affectionate. Second, it is clear that it was Wesley's correspondence as well as his relationships with other women that provoked his wife's jealousy. She accused him of adultery and used his letters to prove her point.

93. John Wesley, *Letters*, 3:208.

94. Ibid., 4:112.

95. Ibid., 4:269.

96. Ibid., 5:62.

97. Ibid., 5:92-93, 124-5.

98. Ibid., 4:61.

99. Maldwyn Edwards, *My Dear Sister: The Story of John Wesley and the Women in His Life* (Manchester: Penwork Ltd., n.d.), 50.

100. John Wesley, *Letters*, 3:239 (Preface to letter).

101. Ibid., 3:244.

102. Ibid., 4:6. Two weeks earlier he had written to Sarah, "Last Friday after many severe words, my wife left me, vowing she would see me no more." He questioned whether he should continue to write to Sarah but after prayer, he believed he should. He continues The Life, "As I had wrote to you the same morning, I began to reason with myself, till I almost doubted whether I had done well in writing or whether I ought to write to you at all. After prayer that doubt was taken away." John Wesley, *Letters*, 4:4.

103. Tyerman, *The Life and Times of the Rev. John Wesley*, 2:110.

104. John Wesley, *Letters*, 5:18.

105. Tyerman, *The Life and Times of the Rev. John Wesley*, 2:109.

106. V.H.H. Green, *The Young Mr. Wesley: A Study of John Wesley and Oxford* (London: Edward Arnold Publishers LTD., 1961), 214.

107. Ibid., 210.

108. John Wesley, *Letters of the Rev. John Wesley*, ed. John Telford, vol. I (London: The Epworth Press, 1931), 199.

109. Benham, *Memoirs*, 46-47 as quoted in Leger, *John Wesley's Last Love*, 164.

110. The Rev. J.B. Wakeley, *Anecdotes of the Wesleys: Illustrative of Their Character and Personal History* (London: Hodder and Stoughton, 27, Paternoster Row), 133.

111. Tyerman, *The Life and Times of the Rev. John Wesley*, 2:103-104.

112. Mabel Brailsford, *A Tale of Two Brothers*, 165.

113. Marjorie Bowen, *Wrestling Jacob: A Study of the Life of John Wesley and Some Members of the Family* (London: The Religious Book Club, 1938), 287. Wesley wrote a letter to the Bishop of London answering the charge that some women brought to the Bishop regarding immoral relations with "female penitents."

114. Leger, *John Wesley's Last Love*, 5, 6.

115. John Wesley, *Letters*, 4:61-62.

116. Ibid., 23 and also 49 (Letter to Blackwell and Molly).

117. Wesley said concerning Eph. 5:22, "Wives submit yourselves to your own husbands-Unless where God forbids. Otherwise, in all indifferent things, the will of the husband is a law to the wife." John Wesley, *Explanatory Notes on the New Testament*, 2d ed. (London: J. Mason, 1860), 301.

118. John Wesley, *Letters*, 4:89.

119. Ibid., 4:23.

120. Ibid., 49-50. Besides telling her that she was to leave him to his own conscience he wrote to her, "And even if a man acts contrary to good conscience, can you reclaim him by violent methods? Vain thought! 'By force beasts act, and are by force restrained: The human mind by gentle means is gained.' Either by gentle means or by none at all. Or if there be an exception, if a rod be for a fool's back, the wife is not the person who is to use it towards her husband." [Oct. 27, 1758].

121. JW's MSS as quoted in Leger, *John Wesley's Last Love*, 75.

122. Letter to Mary Bosanquet, June 13, 1771, as printed in Paul Wesley Chilcote, *John Wesley and the Women Preachers of Early Methodism* (Metuchen, N.J. and London: The American Theological Library Association and the Scarecrow Press, Inc., 1991), 143.

123. Robert Southey, *The Life of John Wesley* (London: Hutchinson and Co., no copyright), 265-266.

124. Telford, *The Life of John Wesley*, 260-261.

125. Tyerman, *The Life and Times of the Rev. John Wesley*, 2:114.

126. Brailsford, *A Tale of Two Brothers*, 230.

127. Telford, *The Life of John Wesley*, 261.

128. John Wesley, *Letters*, 4:23-24.

129. John Wesley, *Letters*, 4:89.

130. Ibid., 6:274.

131. Tyerman, *John Wesley*, Vol. II, 110.

132. Ibid., 6:476-7.

133. Ibid., 6:100.

134. Ibid., 4:62.

135. Ibid., 6:100-1.

136. Ibid., 4:49 (See also 52-53, and 79-80).

137. Ibid.

138. Ibid., 6:273. See also John Wesley, *Journal*, 6:89.

139. John Wesley, *Letters*, 6:322.

Endnotes

140. Richard Watson, *The Life of the Rev. John Wesley* (New York: B. Waugh and T. Mason, 1832), 189.

141. Daniel Wise, *The Story of a Wonderful Life* (New York: Eaton and Mains, 1873), 227.

142. Robert Southey, *The Life of Wesley: And the Rise and Progress of Methodism*, vol. 2 (London: Oxford University Press, 1925), 153-4.

143. John Wesley, *Letters*, 4:77.

144. Charles Wesley, *Journal*, 2:217.

145. Ibid., 210.

146. John Wesley, *Letters*, June 10, 1774.

147. John Wesley, *Letters*, Oct. 23, 1759.

148. Stanley Ayling, *John Wesley*, 224.

149. John Wesley, *Letters*, 6:99.

150. Charles wrote, "He made it his request to his wife and me, to forget all that is past; which I readily agreed to, and once more offered her my service, in great sincerity. Neither will I suspect hers, but hope she will *do* as she *says*." Charles Wesley, *Journal*, 2:97. See also 2:193. See also Charles' letter to his wife on Dec. 3, 1753. He writes, "My brother entreated me, yesterday, and his wife, to forget all that is past on both sides. I sincerely told him I would, for his as well as Christ's sake. My sister said the same." Charles Wesley, *Journal*, 2:193.

151. Charles Wesley, *Journal*, 2:213.

152. John wrote to Blackwell on April 9, 1755, "Being very fully persuaded that my brother would gladly embrace any overture of peace, I told him almost as soon as we met what my wife had agreed to. He answered not one word. After a day or two I spoke with him again. It had the same success. The Sunday before he left Bristol I desired to speak to him, but he did not come. Just as I was going out of town the next morning he sent me to call at his house. But I could not then; and before I came back he was set out for London, only leaving a note that he had left his answer with Lady Huntingdon. It may be so; but I saw her twice afterwards, and she said nothing of it to me. Neither am I (any more than my wife) willing to refer the matter to her arbitration. From the whole I learn that there is no prospect of peace. When one is willing, then the other flies off. I shall profit by both; but I am sorry to do it at the expense of others." John Wesley, *Works*, 26:553-4.

153. Charles Wesley, *Journal*, 2:201.

154. Ibid.

155. John Wesley, *Letters*, 6:99.

156. Charles Wesley, *Journal*, 2:247.

157. Ibid., 2:260.

158. Henry Moore, *The Life of the Rev. John Wesley*, 2:173.

159. John Wesley, *Letters*.

160. John Wesley, *Letters*, 6:101-2. Charles Wesley's daughter said, "My father used to say that his brother's patience toward his wife exceeded all

bounds. The daughter of Mrs. Wesley was an indubitable witness of his forbearance, and bore her testimony of it; so did many who knew of the treatment which he bore without complaint or reproach." Robert Southey, *The Life of Wesley*, (New York: Harper and Brothers, 1847) 2:154.

161. Ibid., 6:273-4.

162. Henry Moore, *Life of Wesley*, 175.

163. Ibid.

164. On June 30, 1772, John Wesley wrote in his Journal that she is with him. They are at an inn. John spoke to a man while Molly spoke to a woman. John Wesley, *Journal*, 6:474. We know she left him again based on the ensuing correspondence. See John Wesley, *Journal*, 6:273.

165. John Wesley, *Letters*, 6:273-4

166. Ibid., 6:321-2.

167. MS entitled *Life of Benson* as quoted in John Wesley, *Journal*, 6:246.

168. John Wesley, *Journal*, 6:337.

Chapter 2 - The Marriage of George Whitefield

1. Lord Bolingbroke, as quoted on the jacket of George Whitefield, *George Whitefield's Journals* (Edinburgh: The Banner of Truth Trust, 1989; reprint from the 1960 ed.).

2. Nathan Cole, *Spiritual Travels*, as quoted in George Whitefield, *George Whitefield's Journals*, new ed. (Edinburgh: the Banner of Truth Trust, 1960; reprint, n.p., 1756), 562.

3. Benjamin Franklin, *Benjamin Franklin: The Autobiography and Other Works*, Selected and Edited with an Introduction by L. Jesse Lemisch (New York: The New American Library, 1961), 118.

4. John Gillies, *Memoirs of Rev. George Whitefield* (New Haven: Whitmore and Buckingham and H. Mansfield, 1838), 301.

5. John Wesley, "On the Death of Mr. Whitefield," in *The Works of John Wesley*, 3d ed. (Peabody, Massachusetts: Hendrickson Publishers, 1991; reprint, London: Wesleyan Methodist Book Room, 1872), 6:174.

6. Ibid., 6:177.

7. J.C. Ryle, "George Whitefield and His Ministry" in *Select Sermons of George Whitefield* (London: The Banner of Truth Trust, 1958), 11.

8. C. H. Spurgeon as quoted on the jacket of Whitefield, *Journals*.

9. Gillies, Funeral sermon by the Rev. John Newton as cited in *Memoirs*, 253.

10. For example, Cornelius Winter (Gillies, *Memoirs*, 292) and R. Elliot (Ryle, *Select Sermons*, 51).

11. James Paterson Gledstone, *George Whitefield, M.A., Field-Preacher* (New York: American Tract Society, 2nd edition), 347.

12. Written by Thomas Olivers. Ibid., 346.

13. Written by Robert Robinson. Ibid., 347.

14. Written by John Fawcett. Ibid.

15. Gillies, *Memoirs*, 300.

Endnotes

16. Gledstone, *George Whitefield*, 349.

17. Ibid.

18. J.B. Wakeley, *Anecdotes of the Rev. George Whitefield* (London: Hodder and Stoughton, Paternoster Row, 1900) 184.

19. *Anecdotes*, 210.

20. Harry S. Stout, "Heavenly Comet", as quoted in *Christian History: George Whitefield*, issue 38, Vol. XII, No. 2, 10.

21. Gillies, *Memoirs*, 276.

22. Ibid., 261.

23. J. I. Packer, "Great George," *Christianity Today*, 19 September 1986, 12.

24. George Whitefield, *A Select Collection of Letters of the Late Reverend George Whitefield ... From the Year 1734, to 1770. Including the Whole Period of his Ministry. With An Account of The Orphan-House in Georgia, To the Time of his Death*, vol. 3 (London: Printed for Edward and Charles Dilly, in the Poultry; and Messrs. Kincaid and Creech, at Edinburgh, 1772), 72.

25. Ibid., 1:338.

26. Whitefield, *Journal*, 75. He was ordained in June 1736.

27. Whitefield, *Letters*, 3:341.

28. Ibid., 2:51.

29. Whitefield used affectionate terms to describe her, such as "my dear wife," "my dear yoke-fellow," and "my dear companion." Whitefield, *Letters*, 1:448; 2:123; and 1:342. In the only published letter written to her, he addressed her as "My dear Love." Ibid., 1:405. He said they were "two happy pilgrims," and claimed they were "happy in JESUS and happy in one another." Ibid., 2:87. Toward the end of their lives, he mentioned that it will be a pleasure to dine with her. Ibid., 3:366.

30. George Whitefield, "A Prayer for a Woman, desiring Direction of GOD, after an Offer of marriage is made to her," in *The Works of the Reverend George Whitefield. Containing All His Sermons and Tracts Which have been already Published*, vol. 4 (London: Printed for Edward and Charles Dilly, in the Poultry; and Messrs. Kincaid and Creech, at Edinburgh, 1771), 480.

31. Whitefield, "Observations on Select Passages of Scripture Turned into Catechetical Questions," in *The Works*, 4:351.

32. Whitefield, "A Letter to the Religious Societies of England," in *The Works*, 4:24.

33. Whitefield, "A Prayer for a Woman, desiring Direction of GOD," in *The Works*, 4:480.

34. George Whitefield, "The Marriage of Cana," in *Twenty-Three Sermons on Various Subjects* (London: W. Strahan, 1745), 3, microfilm.

35. Whitefield, *Letters*, 1:338.

36. Ibid.

37. Ibid., 1:37.

38. George Whitefield, "A Prayer for a Man, convinced that it is His Duty to marry, for Direction in the Choice of a Wife," in *The Works*, 4:479.

This statement raises the question regarding Whitefield's view of women and whether he viewed women as being seductive. Whitefield believed a man might be blinded by his own "lust or passion" in choosing a wife and would thus choose a wife whom he found to be attractive rather than one who was "after thy (God's) own heart." In this way he would "fall by the hand of a woman." Whether Whitefield viewed woman as seductive is open to further study, however the context in this situation seems to suggest that Whitefield was more concerned with *man's* tendency to be blinded by *his own* lust than that women have seductive powers.

39. Whitefield, *Letters*, 1:159.

40. Ibid., 1:160.

41. Ibid., 4:480.

42. Ibid., 4:479. See also Whitefield, "The Marriage of Cana," 3.

43. Whitefield, "A Prayer for a Woman, desiring Direction of GOD," 4:480.

44. Ibid.

45. George Whitefield, "A Prayer for a Woman lately married to a believing Husband," in *The Works*, 4:478.

46. Ibid.

47. George Whitefield, "Christ the Believer's Husband," in *Five Sermons on the Following Subjects* (London: W. Strahan, 1747), 19, microfilm.

48. Ibid., 21.

49. Ibid., 22.

50. Ibid., 23.

51. Ibid., 25.

52. George Whitefield, "The Great Duty of Family-Religion," in *Twenty-Three Sermons*, 96-97, microfilm.

53. Whitefield, *Letters*, 2:361.

54. Whitefield, "Family-Religion," 96.

55. Ibid., 97.

56. Ibid., 109.

57. Ibid., 97.

58. George Whitefield, "Christ the Support of the Tempted" (London: Printed for C. Whitefield, 1740), 20, microfilm.

59. Whitefield, "Family-Religion."

60. Whitefield, "Family-Religion," 102.

61. Whitefield, "Family-Religion."

62. George Whitefield, "The Observation of the Birth of Christ the Duty of all Christians, or the True Way of Keeping Christmas" (London: Printed for C. Whitefield, 1740), 19, microfilm.

63. Ibid.

64. George Whitefield, "The Great Duty of Charity Recommended, Particularly to All Who Profess Christianity" (London: Printed for C. Whitefield, 1740), 3-4, microfilm.

65. Whitefield, "Observation of the Birth of Christ," 19.

66. Ibid.

67. Ibid., 12.

68. He once wrote to another man, "Should you prove any otherwise than a pious husband, it will be one of the greatest afflictions I ever met with in my life." Whitefield, *Letters*, 2:259.

69. Wesley, "On the Death of Mr. Whitefield," 175.

70. Whitefield, *Letters*, 3:12.

71. Ibid., 1:311.

72. For example, Whitefield, *Letters*, 1:275; 2:136; 2:159; 2:192.

73. Whitefield, *Letters*, 1:15.

74. Whitefield, "God, A Believer's Glory," in Gillies, *Memoirs*, 567.

75. Whitefield, "Family-Religion," 97.

76. George Whitefield, "The Gospel, A Dying Saint's Triumph," in Gillies, *Memoirs*, 542.

77. George Whitefield, *Letters of George Whitefield For the Period 1734-1742* (Edinburgh: The Banner of Truth Trust, 1976; reprinted from *The Works of George Whitefield*, 1771) 131.

78. Whitefield, "God, A Believer's Glory," in Gillies, *Memoirs*, 572.

79. Whitefield, "Walking with God," in *Five Sermons on the Following Subjects* (London: W. Strahan, 1742), 104, microfilm.

80. George Whitefield, "Persecution Every Christian's Lot," in Gillies, *Memoirs*, 353.

81. Whitefield, *Journal*, 37.

82. Ibid., 38.

83. A funeral sermon by the Rev. Mr. Parsons at Newburyport, in Gillies, *Memoirs*, 230-231.

84. Whitefield, *Letters*, Banner of Truth edition, 16.

85. George Whitefield, "The Polite and Fashionable Diversions of the Age Destructive to Soul and Body" (London: Printed for C. Whitefield, 1740), 23, microfilm.

86. Whitefield, *Letters*, 1:99.

87. Ibid., 2:93.

88. Ibid., 1:170.

89. George Whitefield, "Persecution Every Christian's Lot," in *Nine Sermons Upon the Following Subjects* (Edinburgh: T. Lumieden and J. Robertson, 1742), 70, microfilm.

90. Gillies, Appendix, 308.

91. Charles Wesley, "Elegy on Whitefield."

92. Whitefield, *Letters*, 1:33.

93. Gillies, "Whitefield's Will" in the Appendix, 306.

94. Ibid., 2:44.

95. Ibid., 2:48. See also George Whitefield, "Blind Bartimeus," in *Five Sermons on the Following Subjects* (London: W. Strahan, 1747), 63, microfilm.

96. Whitefield, "Blind Bartimeus," 63.

97. Ibid.

98. Whitefield, *Letters*, 1:193.
99. George Whitefield, "The Gospel Supper," in *Five Sermons*, 53.
100. Ibid., 52. His theological rationale developed out of his own experience. This is not to suggest that his view does not have Biblical warrant. I am simply tracing the development of his theology.
101. Whitefield, *Letters*, 3:14.
102. Whitefield, *Journal*, 50.
103. Whitefield, "Charity," 16.
104. Whitefield, *Letters*, 386.
105. Ibid.
106. Ryle, *Select Sermons*, 23.
107. Gillies, *Memoirs*, 276.
108. Whitefield, *Letters*, 3:12.
109. Ibid., 3:94.
110. Ibid., 1:121.
111. Gillies, *Memoirs*, 268.
112. Cornelius Winter in Gillies, Appendix, 294.
113. Gillies, *Memoirs*, 270.
114. Ibid.
115. Ibid., 274.
116. Funeral Sermon of the Rev. Henry Venn as cited in Gillies, *Memoirs*, 274.
117. Whitefield, *Letters*, 3:131.
118. Ibid., 3:147.
119. John Wesley, *The Works of John Wesley*, vol. III, *Journals* (Peabody, Massachusetts: Hendrickson Publishers, 1991; reprint, London: Wesleyan Methodist Book Room, 1872), 238.
120. For example, see Whitefield, *Letters*, 2:251; 3:18.
121. Ibid., 2:217. He was only thirty-four years old at the time!
122. Ibid., 3:151.
123. Ibid., 3:155.
124. Ibid., 3:229.
125. Ibid., 2:126.
126. Ibid., 2:125.
127. Ibid., 3:20; 3:151; and 3:271.
128. Gillies, *Memoirs*, 245.
129. Cornelius Winter as cited in Ibid., 295.
130. Ryle, *Select Sermons*, 29.
131. Gillies, *Memoirs*, 264.
132. The Rev. Augustus Montague Toplady, in Gillies, Appendix, 299.
133. Ibid., 2:449; 3:39; 3:244. He once wrote, "Glad should I be to travel for Jesus all the year round. It is more to me than my necessary food." Ibid., 3:36.
134. Ibid., 3:48; 3:59.
135. Ibid., 3:54.
136. Ibid., 3:32.

137. Ibid., 2:415. See also 3:334. The first reference was written midway through his ministry. The latter reference was written four years before he died.

138. Stout, "Heavenly Comet," 14.

139. Whitefield, *Letters*, 3:351.

140. John Wesley, "On the Death of Mr. Whitefield," 6:174.

141. Gillies, *Memoirs*, 284.

142. Whitefield, *Letters*, 3:24.

143. Ibid., 3:68.

144. John Wesley, "On the Death of Mr. Whitefield," 6:175.

145. He wrote, "I think I can say, 'The love of CHRIST constrains me.'" Whitefield, *Letters*, 2:276.

146. Whitefield, "Charity," 16.

147. Whitefield, *Letters*, 1:296.

148. John Wesley's funeral sermon as cited in Gillies, *Memoirs*, 246.

149. Ibid., 245.

150. Ibid., 246.

151. Gillies, *Memoirs*, 47.

152. Ibid.

153. George Whitefield, *Letters*, Banner of Truth edition, 377.

154. Ibid., 384.

155. Whitefield, *Letters*, 2:295.

156. Ibid., 2:341.

157. Ibid., 1:355.

158. Ibid., 1:1. This was the first published letter.

159. Ibid., 2:39.

160. Ibid., 2:50.

161. Ibid., 2:51.

162. Ibid., 2:50.

163. Ibid., 2:51.

164. Ibid., 2:52.

165. Ibid.

166. Ibid.

167. Ibid.

168. A recent biography of Whitefield suggests that while Whitefield was deeply passionate regarding his public life and ministry, in his private life he was merely proper but never impassioned. This episode regarding the death of Whitefield's son is used as one example in painting this picture of Whitefield. Harry S. Stout, *The Divine Dramatist: George Whitefield and the Rise of Modern Evangelicalism* (Grand Rapids, Michigan: William B. Eerdmans Publishing Company, 1991), 170. While this episode does reveal the priority that Christ and his ministry had in his life, this is not to suggest that Whitefield was cold and unfeeling. Whitefield felt deep grief over his son's death, yet he did continue on in ministry.

169. Ibid., 1:158.

170. Ibid., 1:158.

171. Ibid., 1:182.

172. Ibid., 1:338.

173. Ibid., 1:363.

174. Ibid., 1:344.

175. Ibid., 1:363.

176. Ibid.

177. Ibid.

178. Arnold A. Dallimore, *George Whitefield: The Life and Times of the Great Evangelist of the Eighteenth-Century Revival*, vol. 2 (Edinburgh: The Banner of Truth Trust, 1989; reprint), 103.

179. Ibid., 104.

180. Ibid., 108.

181. Ibid., 113.

182. Whitefield, *Letters*, 1:242.

183. Ibid., 3:71.

184. Ibid., 3:341.

185. Ibid., 2:450.

186. Ibid., 2:83.

187. Ibid., 2:50.

188. Selected Trevecka Letters, (1742-1747) as quoted in Dallimore, *Life and Times*, 2:206.

189. Whitefield, *Letters*, 1:159.

190. Ibid., 1:160.

191. Ibid., 1:161.

192. Ibid., 1:194.

193. Ibid., 1:194.

194. Ibid., 1:194.

195. Ibid., 1:245.

196. Ibid., 1:194.

197. Ibid.

198. Ibid.

199. George Whitefield, "Christ the Best Husband: Or an Invitation to Young Women to Come and See Christ" (London: Printed for C. Whitefield, 1740), 23, microfilm.

200. It must be stated that they did not have a lengthy courtship. Whitefield apparently knew her for a while and knew of her proven worth.

201. Whitefield, *Letters*, 1:194.

202. Whitefield, *Journal*, 477.

203. He addressed women as Mrs., Miss, or by some other formal title. Only once in his published letters do we see any hint of an affectionate attitude. He wrote to Mrs. Ann D.-, "My very dear Sister, They (her letters) increased that love, which I had before to the writer of them." Whitefield, *Letters*, 1:449.

204. Ibid., 1:468.

205. Ibid., 1:118.

206. Wesley, "On the Death of Mr. Whitefield," 176.
207. Mrs. E. Benyon, "Mrs. James, Abergavenny, Her Courtship with Howell Harris and her Marriage to George Whitefield," WPHS Journal XXVIII, No. 1, 12 as quoted in Dallimore, *Life and Times*, 102.
208. Dallimore, *Life and Times*, 102.
209. Wesley, *Journal*, 1:339.
210. M. H. Jones, *The Trevecka Letters* (Caernarvon, 1932), 235-6 as quoted in Dallimore, *Life and Times*, 102-3.
211. Dallimore, *Life and Times*, 103.
212. Benyon, *Journal*, 19 as quoted in Dallimore, *Life and Times*, 107.
213. Ibid.
214. Tom Benyon, ed. *Howell Harris, Reformer and Soldier* (Caernarvon: Calvinistic Methodist Bookroom, 1958), 37, as quoted in Dallimore, *Life and Times*, 112.
215. Whitefield, *Letters*, 2:97. Compare this to Wesley's comment regarding what it was like to travel with his wife.
216. PHS Journal, Vol. XXXII, p. 76 as quoted in Dallimore, *Life and Times*, 2:214.
217. Ibid., 2:201.
218. Ibid., 2:77.
219. Ibid., 2:25.
220. Ibid., 2:77.
221. T. Benyon, *Howell Harris*, 37 as quoted in Dallimore, *Life and Times*, 112.
222. Whitefield, *Letters*, 2:68.
223. Compiled by Joseph Belcher, *George Whitefield: A Biography, with Special Reference to His Labors in America* (New York: American Tract Society) 136.
224. George Whitefield, *Letters*, Banner of Truth edition, 452.
225. Whitefield, *Letters*, 2:84.
226. Ibid., 2:85.
227. Ibid., 3:71.
228. Whitefield, "Christ the Best Husband," 13.
229. Ibid., 14.
230. Ibid., 17.
231. Whitefield, *Letters*, 3:372-3.
232. Ibid., 3:372-3. This is a Biblical allusion to Sarah in Genesis.
233. He wrote, "let every, even the most beloved Isaac, be immediately sacrificed for God." Ibid., 2:348. See also George Whitefield, "Abraham Offering up his Son Isaac," in *Twenty-Three Sermons on Various Subjects* (London: Printed by W. Strahan, 1745), 64-65, microfilm.
234. Ibid., 2:87.
235. Ibid., 3:377.
236. Wesley, "On the Death of Mr. Whitefield," 6:174.
237. Ibid.

Chapter 3 - The Legacy of Jonathan Edwards

1. Sereno Edwards Dwight, *The Life of President Edwards* (New York: S. Converse, 1829), 582.

2. William J. Petersen, "Sarah and Jonathan Edwards: An Uncommon Union," *Partnership* (May-June 1987), 41.

3. E.A. Winship, "The Human Legacy of Jonathan Edwards," *World's Work* (October 1903) as quoted in Ralph G. Turnball, *Jonathan Edwards The Preacher* (Grand Rapids, Michigan: Baker Book House, 1958), 153.

4. Jonathan Edwards, "Sarah Pierrepont," in *Jonathan Edwards: Basic Writings*, ed. Ola Elizabeth Winslow (New York: The New American Library, 1966), 66-67.

5. Petersen, "An Uncommon Union," 42.

6. Dwight, *Life of Edwards*, 113.

7. Ibid., 115.

8. Sereno E. Dwight, "Memoirs of Jonathan Edwards," in *The Works of Jonathan Edwards*, ed. Edward Hickman, (Edinburgh: The Banner of Truth Trust, 1990; reprint, 1974 ed.), 1:xlvi.

9. Ibid.

10. Ibid., 1:xix, xlix.

11. Ibid., 1:xlix.

12. Ibid., 1:xlvi.

13. Dwight, *Life of Edwards*, 114.

14. Dwight, "Memoirs," in *The Works of Jonathan Edwards*, 1:xivi.

15. Dwight, *Life of Edwards*, 172.

16. Dwight, "Memoirs," in *The Works of Jonathan Edwards*, 1:xlv.

17. Ibid., 1:xliv.

18. Ibid., 1:xlv.

19. Iain H. Murray, *Jonathan Edwards: A New Biography* (Edinburgh: Banner of Truth Trust, 1988; reprint), 199.

20. Ibid., 393.

21. Dwight, *Life of Edwards*, 114.

22. Dwight, "Memoirs," in *The Works of Jonathan Edwards*, 1:xlvi.

23. Ibid.

24. Ibid.

25. Rita Mancha, "The Woman's Authority: Calvin to Edwards," *Journal of Christian Reconstruction* 6 (Winter 1979-80): 98.

26. Petersen, "An Uncommon Union," 44.

27. Murray, *Jonathan Edwards: A New Biography*, 184.

28. Sereno E. Dwight, *Memoirs of Jonathan Edwards*, in *The Works of President Edwards*, vol. 1 (New York: Leavitt, Trow & Co., 1849), 26.

29. Jonathan Edwards, "Christian Cautions; or, the Necessity of Self-Examination," in *The Works of Jonathan Edwards*, p. 183.

30. Ibid.

31. George Whitefield, *George Whitefield's Journals* (Edinburgh: The Banner of Truth Trust, 1989; reprint, March 1960), 477.

32. Ibid.

Endnotes

33. Petersen, "An Uncommon Union," 43.
34. Dwight, *The Life of President Edwards*, 111.
35. Petersen, "An Uncommon Union," 43.
36. Murray, *Jonathan Edwards: A New Biography*, 185.
37. Ibid., 186.
38. Dwight, *The Life of President Edwards*, 285.
39. Ibid., 525.
40. Dwight, "Memoirs," in *The Works of Jonathan Edwards*, 1:186.
41. Dwight, "Memoirs," in *The Works of President Edwards*, 1:27-29.
42. George Whitefield, *Journals*, 476.
43. Dwight, "Memoirs," in *The Works of President Edwards*, 1:27-29.
44. Murray, *Jonathan Edwards: A New Biography*, 192.
45. Dwight, "Memoirs," in *The Works of President Edwards*, 1:27-29.
46. Jonathan Edwards, "Christian Cautions," in *The Works of Jonathan Edwards*, 2:182-183.
47. Ibid., 2:183.
48. Ibid.
49. Dwight, "Memoirs," in *The Works of President Edwards*, 1:30.
50. Dwight, *The Life of President Edwards*, 128.
51. Dwight, "Memoirs," in *The Works of President Edwards*, 1:38.
52. Jonathan Edwards, "Farewell Sermon," in *Jonathan Edwards: Basic Writings*, selected and edited by Ola Winslow (New York: The New American Library, 1966), 179.
53. Dwight, "Memoirs," in *The Works of Jonathan Edwards*, 1:clxxix.
54. Ibid., 1:xciv.
55. Murray, *Jonathan Edwards: a New Biography*, 446.
56. Ibid.
57. Ibid.
58. Murray, *Jonathan Edwards: A New Biography*, 192.
59. Esther Edwards Burr, *The Journal of Esther Edwards Burr, 1754-1757*, ed. Carol F. Karlsen and Laurie Crumpacker (New Haven: Yale University Press, 1984), 224.
60. Ibid., 295-7.
61. Dwight, *The Life of President Edwards*, 571.
62. Ibid., 580.
63. Jonathan Edwards, "The Concern of a Watchman for Souls," in *The Minister's Task and Calling in the Sermons of Jonathan Edwards* by Helen Westra (Lewiston, N.Y.: The Edwin Mellen Press, 1986), 274.
64. Jonathan Edwards, "Christ the Example of Ministers," in *The Works of Jonathan Edwards*, ed. Edward Hickman, vol. 2 (Edinburgh: The Banner of Truth Trust, 1990; reprint, 1974 ed.), 962.
65. Dwight, "Memoirs of Jonathan Edwards," in *The Works of Jonathan Edwards*, 1:xxxix.
66. Jonathan Edwards, "Resolutions," in *The Works of Jonathan Edwards*, 1:xxi.
67. Jonathan Edwards, "Thoughts on the Revival of Religion in New

England" in *The Works of Jonathan Edwards*, 1:375.

68. Dwight, "Memoirs," in *The Works of Jonathan Edwards*, 1:cxc.

69. Ibid., 1:xlv-xlvi.

70. Ibid.

71. Burr, *Journal*, 156.

72. Edwards, "Diary," in *The Works of Jonathan Edwards*, 1:xxxvii.

73. Jonathan Edwards, "Letter to Mr. Probe," in *The Works of Jonathan Edwards*, 1:cvii.

74. Jonathan Edwards, *The Nature of True Virtue*, in *The Works of Jonathan Edwards*, 1:129.

75. Jonathan Edwards, "Christian Cautions, or, The Necessity of Self-Examination," in *The Works of Jonathan Edwards*, 2:184.

76. Edwards, *Thoughts on Revival*, in *The Works of Jonathan Edwards*, 1:387.

77. Ibid.

78. Helen Westra, *The Minister's Task and Calling in the Sermons of Jonathan Edwards* (Lewiston, N.Y.: The Edwin Mellen Press, 1986), 16.

79. Jonathan Edwards, "Christ the Example of Ministers," in *The Works of Jonathan Edwards*, 2:961-962.

80. Jonathan Edwards, "The True Excellency of a Gospel Minister," in *The Works of Jonathan Edwards*, 2:957.

81. "Life of Edwards", Edinburgh edition, 45-46, as quoted in *The Works of Samuel Hopkins* (New York: Garland Publishing, Inc., 1987) vol. 1.

82. Dwight, "Memoirs," in *The Works of Jonathan Edwards*, 1:xiii.

83. Jonathan Edwards, "The Christian Pilgrim," in *The Works of Jonathan Edwards*, 2:246.

84. Jonathan Edwards, "Memoirs," in *The Works of Jonathan Edwards*, 1:xiii.

85. Ibid., 1:xiv.

86. Jonathan Edwards, "The Excellency of Christ," in *The Works of Jonathan Edwards*, 1:688.

87. Westra, *The Minister's Task and Calling*, 19.

88. Edwards, "Thoughts on Revival", in *The Works of Jonathan Edwards*, 1:387.

89. Edwards, "Christ the Example of Ministers," in *The Works of Jonathan Edwards*, 2:963.

90. Edwards, "Watchman," in *The Minister's Task and Calling*, 267.

91. Edwards, "Thoughts on Revival," in *The Works of Jonathan Edwards*, 1:387.

92. Edwards, Page 814 of the interleaved Bible in the Beinicke Edwards MSS Collection, in Westra, *The Minister's Task and Calling*, 26.

93. Westra, *The Minister's Task and Calling*, 20.

94. Westra, Unpublished sermon on Luke 11:27-28, in *The Minister's Task and Calling*, 88.

95. Westra, *The Minister's Task and Calling*, 58.

96. Jonathan Edwards, "The True Excellency of a Gospel Minister," in *The Works of President Edwards*, vol. 3 (New York: Leavitt, Trow & Co.,

1849), 591.

97. Westra, *Minister's Task and Calling*, 69.

98. Edwards, "Thoughts on Revival," in *The Works of Jonathan Edwards*, 1:387.

99. Jonathan Edwards, "Farewell Sermon," in *Basic Writings*, selected, edited, and with a foreword by Ola Elizabeth Winslow (London: The New American Library, 1966), 77.

100. Edwards, "Watchman," in *The Minister's Task and Calling*, 278.

101. He wrote, "It will be our great honour that we are called to this work of Christ, if therein we follow him: for therein we shall be like the Son of God: but if we are unfaithful in this office, and do not imitate our Master, our offence will be heinous in proportion to the dignity of our office, and our final and everlasting disgrace and ignominy proportionably great; and we, who in honour are exalted up to heaven, shall be cast down proportionably low in hell." Edwards, "Christ the Example," in *The Works of Jonathan Edwards*, 2:964. Elsewhere he wrote, "But if we fail of the proper excellency of ministers of the gospel, we shall not be in the sight of God the more worthy or honourable for our high office, but the more abominable and inexcusable; for our wickedness being aggravated by God's great goodness and condescension to us, and the peculiar obligations that he laid upon us; and instead of being eminently beneficial and great blessings, as lights to reflect the beams of Christ's glory and love, we shall be so much the more hurtful and pernicious, for our being in such a station; and so shall be likely hereafter to suffer a so much more dreadful punishment. The devils in hell are so much the more odious to God, and more the objects of his wrath, because he set them in the dignity and glory of angels, the excellency of which state they are fallen from. And it is likely that those in hell that will be nearest to the fallen angels, in their state of misery, will be those that Christ once set to be angels of the churches, but through their unfaithfulness, failed of their proper excellency and end." Edwards, "The True Excellency of a Gospel Minister," in *The Works of Jonathan Edwards*, 2:959.

102. Westra, *unpublished sermon on Luke 10:17,18*, 138.

103. Ibid., 135.

104. Ibid., 137.

105. Helen Petter Westra, "Above All Others: Jonathan Edwards and the Gospel Ministry," *American Presbyterians* 67 (Fall 1989): 209.

106. Edwards, "The Sorrows of the Bereaved Spread Before Jesus," in *The Works of Jonathan Edwards*, 2:967.

107. Ibid.

108. Westra, *The Minister's Task and Calling*, 183.

109. Jonathan Edwards, "The Church's Marriage to Her Sons, and to Her God," in *The Works of Jonathan Edwards*, 2:18.

110. Ibid., 2:20.

111. Ibid., 2:19.

112. Ibid.

113. Ibid., 2:20-21.

114. Jonathan Edwards, "A Commentary on Hebrews," in John H. Gerstner, *The Rational and Biblical Theology of Jonathan Edwards*, vol. 1 (Powhatan, Va.: Berea Publications, 1991), 396.

115. Ibid., 1:401.

116. Ibid., 1:396.

117. Ibid.

118. Ibid., 1:408.

119. Jonathan Edwards, "Charity and Its Fruits," in *Jonathan Edwards: Ethical Writings*, ed. Paul Ramsey (New Haven: Yale University Press, 1989), 372.

120. Jonathan Edwards, "The Nature of True Virtue" in *Jonathan Edwards: Ethical Writings*, 605.

121. Ibid.

122. Ibid., 604.

123. Edwards, "The Church's Marriage," in *The Works of Jonathan Edwards*, 2:20.

124. Ibid., 2:21.

125. Ibid., 2:20.

126. Ibid., 2:20.

127. Ibid., 2:21.

128. Edwards, "Christian Cautions," *The Works of Jonathan Edwards*, 2:183. A description of what Edwards saw to be a good marriage was given in a sermon entitled, "The Sorrows of the Bereaved Spread Before Jesus." To the widow, the one "who stood in the nearest relation to any to the deceased," he said, "God has now taken from you that servant of his, that was the nearest and best friend you had in this world, that was your wise and prudent guide, your affectionate and pleasant companion, who was so great a blessing while he lived, to you and your family, and, under Christ, was so much the comfort and support of your life." To the children he said, "you will no longer have your father's wisdom to guide you, his tender love to comfort and delight you, and his affectionate care to guard you and assist you, and his pious and judicious counsels to direct you, and his holy examples set before you, and his fervent, humble, believing prayers with you and for you." Edwards, "The Sorrows of the Bereaved Spread Before Jesus," 2:968.

129. Edwards, "Resolution #62," 1:22.

130. Daniel Yankelovich, *New Rules:Searching for Self-Fulfillment in a World Turned Upside Down* (New York: Bantam Books, 1981), 8.

131. St. Augustine, *Confessions*, Book I.i.

132. Jonathan Edwards, "Sermon to the Children, August, 1740," in Sandford Fleming, *Children and Puritanism* (New York: The Arno Press and The New York Times, 1969), 100.

133. Jonathan Edwards, *The Works of Jonathan Edwards*, vol. 3 (New York: 1881), 340.

134. In a sermon where Edwards exhorts the believer to examine himself, he asked, "Do you take pains in any measure proportionate to the importance of the matter? You cannot but own that it is a matter of vast importance, that your children be fitted for death, and saved from hell; and that all possible care be taken that it be done speedily; for you know not how soon your children may die." Edwards, "Christian Cautions," in *The Works of Jonathan Edwards*, 2:183.

135. Dwight, *Life of Edwards*, 165-7.

136. Jonathan Edwards, "Theological Questions," in *The Works of Jonathan Edwards*, 1:691.

137. Richard Flinn, "The Puritan Family and the Christian Economy," *Christian Reconstruction* 6 (Winter 1979-80): 75.

138. Jonathan Edwards, "God's Awful Judgment in the Breaking and Withering of the Strong Rods of a Community," in *The Works of Jonathan Edwards*, 2:38.

139. William J. Scheick, *The Writings of Jonathan Edwards: Theme, Motif, and Style* (College Station, Texas: Texas A & M University Press, 1975), 41.

140. Edwards, *True Virtue*, 1:129. Elsewhere he wrote, "God requires of us, that we exercise the utmost watchfulness and diligence in his service. Reason teaches, that it is our duty to exercise the utmost care, that we may know the mind and will of God, and our duty in all the branches of it, and to use our utmost diligence in everything to do it; because the service of God is the great business of our lives, it is that work which is the end of our beings; and God is worthy, that we should serve him to the utmost of our power in all things." Edwards, "Christian Cautions," in *The Works of Jonathan Edwards*, 2:174.

141. Edwards, "The Church's Marriage," in *The Works of Jonathan Edwards*, 2:20.

142. Ibid., 2:20.

143. Ibid., 2:21.

144. Flinn, "The Puritan Family," 82.

145. Janet Fishburn, "The Family as a Means of Grace in American Theology," *Religious Education* 78 (Winter 1983): 91-93.

146. Edwards, "Farewell Sermon", in *The Works of Jonathan Edwards*, 1:ccvi.

147. Flinn, "The Puritan Family," 83.

148. Edwards, "Farewell Sermon," in *The Works of Jonathan Edwards*, 1:ccvi.

149. Margo Todd, "Humanists, Puritans, and the Spiritualized Household," *Church History* 49 (March 1980): 23.

150 Richard A. S. Hall, *The Neglected Northampton Texts of Jonathan Edwards: Edwards on Society and Politics* (Lewiston, N.Y.: The Edwin Mellen Press, 1990), 273.

151. Edwards, "Farewell Sermon," in *The Works of Jonathan Edwards*, 1:ccvi.

152. Flinn, "The Puritan Family," 84-85.

153. Fishburn, "The Family as a Means of Grace," 92.

154. Flinn, "The Puritan Family," 79.

155. Jonathan Edwards, "A Faithful Narrative of a Surprising Work of God," in *The Works of Jonathan Edwards*, 1:346-7.

156. Ibid., 1:347.

157. Edwards, "Christian Cautions," in *The Works of Jonathan Edwards*, 2:185.

158. Ibid., 2:182.

159. Jonathan Edwards, "Great Care Necessary, Lest We Live in Some Way of Sin," as quoted in Scheick, *The Writings of Jonathan Edwards*, 41.

160. Jonathan Edwards, "The Church's Marriage to Her Sons, and to Her God," in *The Works of Jonathan Edwards*, 2:20-21.

161. Edwards, "Christian Cautions," in *The Works of Jonathan Edwards*, 2:182.

162. Ibid.

163. Edwards, "Christian Cautions," in *The Works of Jonathan Edwards*, 2:182.

164. This is an expansive subject which goes beyond Edwards' personal theology to the whole theology surrounding the New England dream. This concept goes beyond the scope of this book.

165. Jonathan Edwards, "Charity and Its Fruits," in *Ethical Writings*, 16.

166. Ibid., 12.

167. Ibid., 13.

168. Ibid., 16.

169. Jonathan Edwards, "Christian Pilgrim," in *The Works of Jonathan Edwards*, 2:244.

170. Dwight, "Memoirs," in *The Works of Jonathan Edwards*, 1:clxxviii.

171. Burr, *Journal*, 301.

172. Dwight, *Life of Edwards*, 579. Emphasis added.

Conclusion
1. Pastor Dwight Edwards of Grace Bible Church in College Station, Texas, and Dr. John Woodbridge, Research Professor of Church History at Trinity Evangelical Divinity School in Deerfield, Illinois.

2. John H. Armstrong, *Five Great Evangelists* (Geanies House, Fearn, Ross-shire, Great Britain: Christian Focus Publications, 1997), 228.

3. Iain H. Murray, *Jonathan Edwards: A New Biography* (Edinburgh: The Banner of Truth Trust, 1988; reprint, 1987), 355.

4. Billy Graham, *Just As I Am: The Autobiography of Billy Graham* (New York: HarperCollins Publishers, 1997), 702-703.

5. Ibid., 709.

6. Elizabeth Isichei, "The Man with Three "Wives"," *Christian History* 56 (Vol. XVI, No. 4), 30.

7. Ibid.

8. John Piper, "Foreword – For Single Men and Women (and the Rest of Us)" in John Piper and Wayne Grudem, eds., *Recovering Biblical Manhood and Womanhood: A Response to Evangelical Feminism* (Wheaton, Illinois:

Crossway Books, 1991), xx.

9. Rhena Taylor, *Single and Whole* (Downers Grove, IL: InterVarsity Press, 1984), 71, as quoted in John Piper, "For Single Men and Women (and the Rest of Us)," xx.

10. Robertson McQuilkin, *The Great Omission* (Grand Rapids, Michigan: Baker Book House, 1984), 87-88.

11. As quoted in Charles Bridges, *The Christian Ministry* (Edinburgh: The Banner of Truth Trust, 1991; reprint from the 1967 ed.), 170.

12. J. Oswald Sanders, *Spiritual Leadership* (Chicago: Moody Press, 1980), 57.

13. Newsletter of Ravi Zacharias International Ministries, June 2003.

14. Charles Bridges, *The Christian Ministry*, 170.

15. Will Durant, *The Life of Greece*, in *The Story of Civilization* vol. 2 (New York: Simon and Schuster, 1966; reprint of 1939 ed.), 269.

16. As quoted in Jon Hinkson's tribute written in honor of his father, Bud Hinkson. August 10, 2002 was the tenth anniversary of his father's going home to be with the Lord.

17. Robertson McQuilkin, *The Great Omission*, 92.

18. Elisabeth Elliot, *Let Me Be a Woman* (Wheaton, Illinois: Tyndale House Publishers, Inc., 1981), 26.

19. Jon Hinkson's tribute to his father, Bud Hinkson. My husband and I ministered at Stanford University with Jon's sister, Joi. Joi is now married and ministers overseas with her husband Roy and their children.

20. Dolina MacCuish, *Luther and His Katie* (Christian Focus Publications Ltd, n.d.), 43-44.

21. Ibid., 44.

22. Elisabeth Elliot, *Let Me Be a Woman*, 52.

23. Jean Fleming, *A Mother's Heart* (Colorado Springs, CO: NavPress, 1982), 215.

24. Gail MacDonald, *High Call, High Privilege*,

25. Dolina MacCuish, *Luther and His Katie*, 48.

26. Martin Luther, *Table Talk*, as quoted in J. H. Alexander, *Ladies of the Reformation* (n.p., n.d.), 80.

27. John R. Mott, "Lessons I Have Learnt in Over Fifty Years of Helping to Establish National and World-wide Movements." I am indebted to whoever gave me this handout.

28. J. Oswald Sanders, *Spiritual Leadership*, 57-58.

29. Jonathan Edwards, "Resolutions," xxi.

30. Jonathan Edwards, "Farewell Sermon," in *Jonathan Edwards: Basic Writings*, selected and edited by Ola Winslow (New York: The New American Library, 1966), 179.

31. Thank you to my husband, Dave, for this insight.

Other Books
of Interest
from
Christian Focus

FIVE GREAT & EVANGELISTS

PREACHERS OF REAL REVIVAL...

- JOHN WESLEY
- GEORGE WHITEFIELD
- ASAHEL NETTLETON
- DUNCAN MATHESON
- HOWELL HARRIS

JOHN H. ARMSTRONG

Five Great Evangelists

John Wesley - George Whitefield
Asahel Nettleton - Duncan Matheson - Howell Harris

John H. Armstrong

True revival changes not just the church but also the society in which people live. The effects of the preaching of the evangelists was felt on both sides of the Atlantic over a 200 year period - they had a formative effect on the sort of society that we are today.

'Refreshingly honest in its accounts as it is edifying. John gives us heroes without airbrushing out their foibles.'

**Michael Horton, Chairman,
Alliance of Confessing Evangelicals**

'A reminder of how far we have drifted from the days when theology mattered and integrity was indispensable for mininstry.'

**Erwin Lutzer, Senior Pastor,
Moody Church, Chicago**

'In this new 'Reader's Digest' version of the lives of five great evangelists, John Armstrong has done an important service. My prayer is that these thrilling stories will stir a new generation.'

John Blanchard, Evangelist

John Armstrong spent 21 years as a pastor and is now President of Reformation and Revival Ministries which seeks to encourage biblical preaching and evangelism.

ISBN 1 85792 157 7

A Call to United,
Extraordinary Prayer...

('An humble attempt...')

Jonathan Edwards

'I can't think of a better way to get one's heart beating in
rhythm with the Father's....' Joni Eareckson Tada

A Call to United, Extraordinary Prayer...

('An humble attempt...')

Jonathan Edwards

Introduced by David Bryant of 'Concerts of Prayer International', the 'American National Prayer Committee' and 'Proclaim Hope'.

This classic book was first published under the title 'An humble attempt to promote explicit agreement and visible union of God's people in extraordinary prayer for the revival of religion and the advancement of Christ's Kingdom'

'As I read the manuscript, faith was birthed in my own heart; faith that in response to focused and united prayer, God might yet do a mighty work in our day.'
Erwin W. Lutzer

'Pick this book up and you will not be able to put it down!'
Raleigh B. Washington

'Too often Prayer is a small, dusty compartment of our lives. This book shows that if we really believe that Prayer is communicating with all powerful, holy, loving and just God - then it will be - it has to be - something entirely different.'
Luis Palau

'I can't think of a better way to get one's heart beating in rhythm with the Savior's....'
Joni Eareckson Tada

ISBN 1 85792 860 1

The Life & Spirituality of

WILLIAM · WILBERFORCE

VITAL
CHRISTIANITY

MURRAY · ANDREW · PURA

Vital Christianity

The Life and Spirituality of William Wilberforce

Murray Andrew Pura

'Some books, said Bacon, should be tasted (and then left), some swallowed (that is, read casually), and "some few chewed and digested," that is read through with care and thought. This book flows so smoothly that it could easily be swallowed, but with Christian role-models of stature currently in such short supply I believe it belongs in Bacon's third class; and it is as such that I recommend it to you.'

J.I Packer

In his early days, Wilberforce's(1759-1833) opposition towards slavery was not a popular position. But Wilberforce was convinced that slavery was an evil that needed to eradicated, and despite fighting against the flow of popular opinion of his time his wish for its abolition was finally fulfilled, a mere three days before his death.

What would have happened if William Wilberforce had followed the conventional wisdom of today and kept his religious beliefs separate from his political opinions?

What would have happened if William Wilberforce had allowed the desire to be relevant, tolerant or popular outweigh any desire to stand for what was right?

This is a fascinating look at William Wilberforce's life. The energy, persistence and unashamedly evangelical faith is a shining example to all Christians today.

Murray Andrew Pura is author of a number of books and pastors a Southern Baptist Church in Pincher Creek, Alberta, Canada.

ISBN 1 85792 916 0

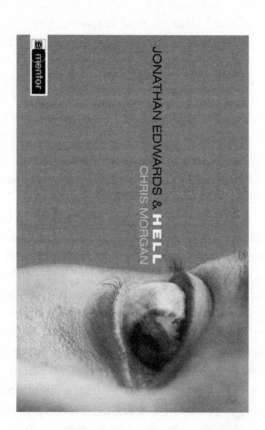

JONATHAN EDWARDS & **HELL**

CHRIS MORGAN

mentor

Jonathan Edwards and Hell

Chris Morgan

In this timely book Chris Morgan gives an overview to the Annihilationist debate, summarising the positions of the protagonists of both sides, and showing how Jonathan Edwards provided the best model for refuting the Annihilationist position.

'In recent years no one has adequately brought to bear the biblical doctrine of God on the doctrine of hell but Jonathan Edwards previously did that very thing. Morgan shows how Edwards successfully responded to the annihilationist arguments of his own day and, he argues, persuasively in my estimation, that Edwards's approach needs to be heard today.'

Robert A. Peterson,
Covenant Theological Seminary, St. Louis

'Jonathan Edwards' doctrines of God and of sin are of profound significance for refuting the case for the annihilation of the unsaved. Christopher Morgan's comprehensive survey of the annihilation debate and his clear exposition of Edwards' views are a valuable resource for those defending biblical teaching regarding eternal punishment.'

David McKay,
Reformed Theological College, Belfast

Chris Morgan is Associate Dean and Professor of Theology at California Baptist University and is Senior Pastor of First Baptist Church of Barstow, California.

ISBN 1 85792 917 9

GEOFFREY HANKS

70Great
CHRISTIANS

The Story of the Christian Church

Peter and Paul, Polycarp, Tertullian, Eusebius, Augustine, Patrick, Alfred
the Great, Francis of Assissi, Wyclif, Luther, Calvin, Knox, Baxter, Bunyan,
Wesley, Hudson Taylor, Livingstone, Slessor, Wilberforce, Muller, Fry,
Booth, Spurgeon, Moody, Lloyd-Jones, Graham, Palau, Carmichael, Nee,
Aylward, Pullinger, Wurmbrand, Saint, Corrie ten Boom...

70 Great Christians

70 Great Christians who Changed the World

Geoffrey Hanks

Throughout the history of the Church there have been people who stand out above the others. It may be for good or bad reasons but for their contemporaries they were 'great' in the sense of 'significant' figures who changed the church of their time.

Geoffrey Hanks skilfully breaks down the main time periods and movements of the Church and shows who were the people who had the most impact on the events taking place. With helpful comparison charts he shows what undercurrents were going on behind the scenes; with enlightening information boxes he throws light on why things turned out the way they did; and throughout you come face to face with the 'movers and shakers' in church history.

Geoffrey Hanks live in England, he is a regular contributor to newspapers and is a respected Church historian and teacher.

ISBN 1 87167 680 0

Christian Focus Publications

publishes books for all ages

Our mission statement –

STAYING FAITHFUL
In dependence upon God we seek to help make His infallible word, the Bible, relevant. Our aim is to ensure that the Lord Jesus Christ is presented as the only hope to obtain forgiveness of sin, live a useful life and look forward to heaven with Him.

REACHING OUT
Christ's last command requires us to reach out to our world with His gospel. We seek to help fulfill that by publishing books that point people towards Jesus and help them develop a Christ-like maturity. We aim to equip all levels of readers for life, work, ministry and mission.

Books in our adult range are published in three imprints.

Christian Focus contains popular works including biographies, commentaries, basic doctrine, and Christian living. Our children's books are also published in this imprint.

Mentor focuses on books written at a level suitable for Bible College and seminary students, pastors, and other serious readers. The imprint includes commentaries, doctrinal studies, examination of current issues, and church history.

Christian Heritage contains classic writings from the past.

For a free catalogue of all our titles, please write to

Christian Focus Publications, Ltd
Geanies House, Fearn,
Ross-shire, IV20 1TW, Scotland, United Kingdom
info@christianfocus.com

For details of our titles visit us on our website
www.christianfocus.com